Y0-AAH-647

AMERICA'S FAVORITE
FLOWERS

AMERICA'S FAVORITE

FLOWERS

David Swift

Gramercy Books
New York

This 2003 edition is published by Gramercy Books, an imprint of Random House Value Publishing, a division of Random House, Inc., New York.

Gramercy is a registered trademark and the colophon is a trademark of Random House, Inc.

Random House
New York • Toronto • London • Sydney • Auckland
www.randomhouse.com

Printed and bound in Italy

All photography supplied by the author

A catalog record for this title is available from the Library of Congress

ISBN 0-517-21849-6

10 9 8 7 6 5 4 3 2 1

Contents

Introduction

It is hard to imagine anything more delightful than flowers or a topic of discussion more guaranteed to lift the spirit and feed the imagination. America not only possesses an abundance of native flowering plants of her own, she has also acquired many from elsewhere which have become deservedly popular and which Americans have well and truly taken to their hearts; all-American favorites quite happily rub shoulders with interesting and striking plants from all over the world.

America has always been generous with her bounty, sending plants and seeds to other countries as well as receiving others in return. One of the first commercial American nurseries was founded in 1737 by William Prince at Flushing Landing on Long Island, where he exported American plants to Europe as well as becoming a major importer. The plant collector John Bartram also had a nursery, which numbered Thomas Jefferson and George Washington among its clients.

There are so many different ways of displaying and enjoying flowers: annuals are invaluable for adding a different and spectacular blaze of color every year, as well as being useful for filling in empty spaces in the herbaceous border, while perennials form the backbone of every garden, flowering reliably year upon year and demanding very little in return.

Any home would be poorer without a few flowers to brighten a sunny window sill or fill a neglected corner. There are flowers suitable for a magnificent display, where personal creativity can be explored to the full, while others might prefer a simple country posy or even a single perfect rose.

During their lifetime, many people are bitten by the collecting bug; this may take various forms, from stamp-collecting to seeking out antique furniture. But remember that the acquisitive passion can also extend to plants – often one particular species which soon takes in all its many varieties. These enthusiasts are the stalwarts of the local flower show and life would be much duller without their single-mindedness and dedication.

It is noticeable, then, that flowers are adaptable and appeal for many different reasons. Not everyone can have a garden but there are still ways of enjoying flowers, even if only in a humble window box or as a pot of hyacinth bulbs, reminding us that spring is at last on its way.

As well as describing plants and suggesting the different ways in which they can be used, this volume also touches upon their medicinal aspects, which is a huge subject in itself, especially nowadays when alternative medicine has never been so popular. It is particularly interesting to realize that plant substances that have been known by herbalists for centuries are around today and still figure in the modern pharmacopoeia, not forgetting the many plants that have been steeped for centuries in folklore and magic. With such interesting facts at our disposal, flowers become an even more fascinating subject!

Zinnia 'Dahlia-Flowered'

Dazzling Annuals

These colorful, resilient and reliable plants are raised each year from seeds sown either outdoors, where they are to flower, or first raised in gentle warmth in a greenhouse or sunroom and later planted outside to create a colorful display. They usually flower throughout summer until the frosts of early fall arrive. Some of them are ideal for planting in beds and borders, others look wonderful in window boxes, hanging baskets, troughs and tubs.

Agrostemma (Caryophyllaceae)

Many annuals which are now popular in America came from other regions of the world and these include the Purple Cockle or Corn Cockle (*Agrostemma githago* 'Milas'), a hardy plant which owes its name to a town in southwestern Turkey where it was first discovered. They appear fragile but are surprisingly resistant to wind and weather. From midsummer to early fall, lilac-pink flowers atop upright stems are revealed, with shading deepening towards the edges of each flower. For an even more spectacular display, position this annual behind scarlet Poppies and red and orange Nasturtiums.

Agrostemma githago 'Milas'

Alyssum maritimum (Lobularia maritimum)

Alyssum (Brassicaceae)

Few garden plants are as well known as Sweet Alyssum (*Lobularia maritima*), earlier and still better known as *Alyssum maritimum.* This hardy annual from Europe and western Asia is usually grown as a half-hardy summer-flowering bedding plant. Throughout summer it bears rounded clusters of white, lilac or purple flowers on neat, bushy but spreading plants.

Apart from its value as an edging for formal beds and borders, it has a country garden appeal when self-sown seedlings are allowed to run riot between paving slabs and alongside rustic paths. However, in formal bedding schemes it usually appears in conjunction with Lobelia and the Scarlet Sage (Salvia).

Amaranthus (Amaranthaceae)

The Tassel Flower or Love-Lies-Bleeding (*Amaranthus caudatus*) is a hardy annual with light-green leaves and long, drooping stems packed with pretty tassels from midsummer to the fall. It is ideal for mixing with Nasturtiums and Marigolds. People who love green flowers, which are superb when used in floral displays

Amaranthus caudatus ('Viridus')

indoors, grow the form 'Viridus,' with its long tassels packed with pale lime-green flowerlets, again from midsummer to fall. As well as introducing interest indoors, it creates a graceful feature in a border when white varieties of snapdragon are positioned in front of it. For even greater effect, *Hosta fortunei* 'Albopicta,' with its pale-green and buff-yellow variegated leaves, can be added to this duo.

Antirrhinum (Scrophulariaceae)

Native to the warm, sunny climate of southern Europe, the Snapdragon (*Antirrhinum majus*) managed to escape and make its home in many cooler parts of Europe, as well as in the United States. Earlier known as Calf's Snout and Lion's Mouth, this hardy perennial is invariably grown as a half-hardy annual in gardens, where it creates a galaxy of colors from white and yellow to pink and red from midsummer to the onset of frost. With their irregularly-shaped flowers, Snapdragons make ideal companions for other plants, including the Flowering Tobacco Plant (*Nicotiana alata*) and Annual Mallow (*Lavatera trimestris*).

Antirrhinum majus

Begonia semperflorens

Begonia (Begoniaceae)

The Wax Begonia, Bedding Begonia or Wax Plant (*Begonia semperflorens*) is a tender perennial invariably grown as a half-hardy annual for planting in summer-flowering displays. Native to South America, this fibrous-rooted plant has earned its place as an essential part of formal planting, creating bushy mounds drenched in flowers from early to late summer. Colors are white, shading through pink and red to scarlet. As well as making a compact edging for paths, it is ideal for planting in containers on a patio. It can also be grown as a pot plant for taking indoors to decorate cool rooms.

Do not confuse the Wax Begonia with the winter-dormant, perennial tuberous- and rhizomatous-rooted Begonias, which have a completely different habit and which need lifting and storing for the winter.

Chrysanthemum (Asteraceae)

Of Moroccan ancestry, the hardy Annual Chrysanthemum (*Chrysanthemum carinatum*), also known as the Tri-Coloured Chrysanthemum, has been adopted throughout the world to enrich summer borders with large, daisy-like, flat-faced flowers with contrasting circular bandings in a medley of colors. It creates such a strong splash of color that it can easily overpower other flowers in a border. Try cohabiting this dazzling annual with the ornamental Squirreltail Barley or Squirreltail Grass (*Hordeum jubatum*), with its densely-tufted nodding panicles.

Cleome (Capparaceae)

The Spider Flower (*Cleome spinosa*) is native to a wide area stretching from southern Mexico to Venezuela and the Caribbean. It is a half-hardy annual with distinctive heads of whiskery flowers throughout summer. The flowers are normally white flushed with pink, though pink, rose, lilac, purple and white varieties are now available. It grows to a height of up to 4 feet and can be used to create height contrasts within annual borders. Alternatively, plant it as a filler in a mixed border.

Consolida (Ranunculaceae)

With its lax and wispy habit, the Annual or Rocket Larkspur (*Consolida ambigua*), earlier and still

Chrysanthemum carinatum

Cleome spinosa

Consolida ambigua

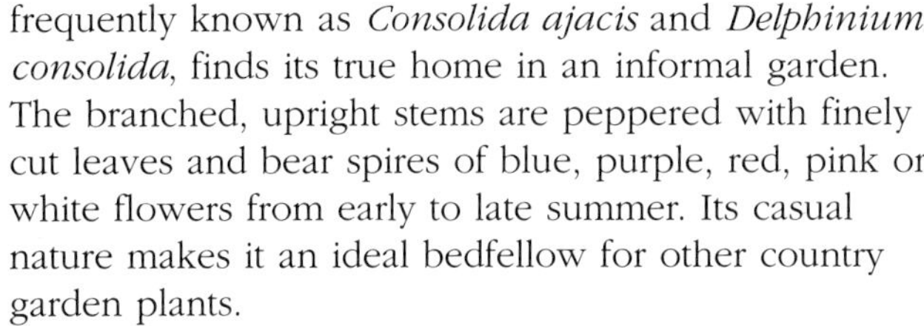

frequently known as *Consolida ajacis* and *Delphinium consolida*, finds its true home in an informal garden. The branched, upright stems are peppered with finely cut leaves and bear spires of blue, purple, red, pink or white flowers from early to late summer. Its casual nature makes it an ideal bedfellow for other country garden plants.

At one time Consolida was widely valued as a dressing for wounds and was claimed to improve sight; in fact it was said that just looking at the flowers made this happen! A tincture made from the seeds was used to kill lice and nits in the hair and the flowers, when combined with alum, were a source of a green dye.

Cosmos (Asteraceae)

The Mexican Daisy or Cosmos (*Cosmos bipinnatus*) is a half-hardy annual with masses of single, dahlia-like, 3–4-inch flowers in colors including white, rose-pink, crimson, orange and yellow from late summer to the onset of the first frosts. It may lack the dramatic shape of its fellow countryman the Spider Flower (Cleome), but it has a delicate daisy shape with flowers borne on

Cosmos bipinnatus

Eschscholzia californica

mid-green, fern-like leaves. Plant it in a narrow border alongside a path so that the glorious flowers can be enjoyed from above.

Eschscholzia (Papaveraceae)

Many annuals have an all-American heritage and perhaps none more so than the California Poppy (*Eschscholzia californica*), a radiant plant which was so widespread in its native California that the Spaniards named the place the "Golden West" and the "Land of Fire." Quite erroneously, these descriptions have been attributed to the discovery of gold in California in 1848, but they more correctly allude to the bright-yellow poppy. The Spaniards dedicated the flower to San Pascual, whose color is yellow, and it was evocatively described as "his altar-cloth spread on the hills." Although now botanically known as Eschscholzia, after the Russian-born naturalist and traveler Johann von Eschscholz (1793–1831), the Spanish retained the lovely old name *Capa d'oro*, meaning gold mantle or cloth of gold. Later it was adopted as the state flower of California. This hardy annual has delicate, finely-cut, blue-green leaves and masses of saucer-shaped, 3-inch-wide bright-orange flowers which appear from early to late summer. Nowadays, there are varieties in scarlet, crimson, rose, orange, yellow, white and red. Try low-growing varieties as a border edging, or mix them in large drifts with other hardy annuals. When using them for room decoration, cut them when the flowers are still in bud.

In earlier times the leaves were used by Native Americans as a vegetable, while medicinally it has been used for the treatment of headaches.

Euphorbia (Euphorbiaceae)

Snow-on-the-Mountain or Ghost Weed (*Euphorbia marginata*) is a hardy annual native to the United States. It has a bushy habit and bright-green leaves that

Euphorbia marginata 'Summer Icicle'

become veined and edged with white as the plant matures. The white flowers are rather insignificant, its attraction being the foliage which, as well as creating a magnificent display in borders, is useful for flower arrangements indoors. After cutting the stems, place them in hot water so that the sap or latex coagulates to prevent it from escaping. This sap was once used by Native Americans in New Mexico as a chewing gum.

Helianthus (Asteraceae)

The Sunflower (*Helianthus annuus*) is especially popular with children. Native to both the United States and Central America as well as to Peru, where it was once held in great esteem as an emblem of the sun god, it is a hardy annual with daisy-like flower heads up to 12 inches wide during mid and late summer. There are many varieties, their heights ranging from 3–10 feet and in color from pale-primrose to copper-brown. Each flower has a central purple or brown disc. It was highly acclaimed by Europeans, who first saw it in 1569 when it was known as the "Hearbe of the Sunne."

Large and beautiful flowers are not the Sunflower's

Helianthus annuus

Heliotropium arborescens

only claim to fame: the nutritious seeds were eaten both raw and roasted by Native Americans (a habit now common everywhere). They also dried and crushed the seeds, mixing them with bone marrow to create an edible paste. The flowers were used to create a dye, while early settlers ate the young flower heads as a vegetable and fed the leaves to their animals.

Try letting children sow seeds of tall, large-flowered varieties up against a wind-sheltered wall. Alternatively, mix moderate-height varieties with color-contrasting annuals such as the Woolflower, *Celosia argentea plumosa.*

Heliotropium (Boraginaceae)

For a flamboyant display choose the popular and widely-famed Heliotrope (*Heliotropium arborescens*), also known as Cherry Pie or Turnsole. This half-hardy perennial from Peru is usually grown as a half-hardy annual for flowering in borders throughout summer. In some catalogs it is still listed as *H. peruvianum* or *H. x hybridum*, which can be confusing; but it is worth

Lavatera trimestris

growing for its fragrant, Forget-Me-Not-like flowers which are mostly dark violet but can also range from lavender to white. In a border, varieties with dark-violet flowers create a dramatic color contrast when planted next to *Senecio cineraria*, the popular Dusty Miller, which reveals deeply-lobed leaves covered with white and woolly hairs that give it a silver appearance. The name Cherry Pie is claimed to indicate the scent of the flowers, although to many they smell of vanilla or almonds, while Turnsole refers to the way the flowers turn to face the sun.

Lavatera (Malvaceae)
The Annual Mallow (*Lavatera trimestris*), also known as *Lavatera rosea*, is another spectacular annual, with a hardy and bushy habit providing masses of rose- or lavender-pink, slightly trumpet-shaped flowers from midsummer to early fall. It is at its most dramatic when grown in a large clump. It is a versatile annual and looks good with several combinations of plants, including purple-leaved Cannas and grey-leaved plants such as Artemisias.

Limnanthes (Limnanthaceae)
The Poached Egg Flower, also commonly known as Meadow Foam and botanically as *Limnanthes douglasii,* soon smothers the ground with white-edged yellow flowers. Native to the United States, it is a hardy annual and year after year gives birth to a myriad of self-sown seedlings which can be pulled out if they are not growing where you want them. Plants are low-growing, so try them in large drifts alongside paths where, as well as creating a feast of color, they will spill over to soften the harsh edges.

Limnanthes douglasii

Linum grandiflorum 'Rubrum'

Linum (Linaceae)
Originally from Algeria, the Scarlet Flax (*Linum grandiflorum* 'Rubrum') creates a showy display with brilliant saucer-shaped crimson flowers throughout summer. Plants grow to a height of 15–18 inches, making them more noticeable than if they were closer to the ground, and consequently making a stronger impact.

Linum grandiflorum, however, has clear rose-colored flowers which are less dramatic than 'Rubrum' and are ideal cohabiting with Nigella or Love-in-a-Mist (page 55). As well as decorating borders, plants can also be grown in pots to provide indoor decoration.

Lobelia (Lobeliaceae)
The Edging Lobelia (*Lobelia erinus*) is one of the most popular garden plants. However, this common name is slightly misleading as there are both trailing and bushy types. In 1759 it arrived in England from the Cape of Good Hope, South Africa, and within a few years was grown in the Chelsea Physic Garden in London. Seeds were taken to America, while in Victorian England in the mid to late 1800s it was gaining widespread popularity in formal bedding schemes. Nowadays, trailing forms are used to decorate hanging baskets and the edges of window boxes in white and shades of blue or red. Bushy forms are used to create decorative edges to borders, and often as companions to Sweet Alyssum (*Lobularia maritima*). When using Lobelia and Alyssum in this way, plant two Lobelia plants to one of Alyssum to allow for the fact that Alyssum grows more vigorously.

Malcolmia (Cruciferae)
The popular name Virginian Stock (*Malcolmia maritima*) implies that it is a plant from the state of Virginia; however, this is not the case and it actually

Lobelia erinus

originated in southern Mediterranean regions. It is easy to grow and when grouped with the Night-Scented Stock (*Matthiola bicornis*), a Greek hardy annual popularly known in the United States as the Evening Stock and Perfume Plant, is ideal for growing under windows or near patio doors.

Myosotis (Boraginaceae)
Of all the flowers, the Forget-Me-Not (*Myosotis sylvatica*) has the most romantic associations. In the language of flowers it implies Remembrance and True Love, while in about 1390 Henry of Lancaster, later to become Henry IV of England, took the flower as his emblem. It was said that those who wore it would never be forgotten by their lovers: there is a legend of a knight clutching at a bank where the flower is growing and plaintively crying "Forget-me-not" to his lady before drowning.

The common Forget-Me-Not is native to Europe, North Africa and western Asia, and is now naturalized

Myosotis sylvatica

Malcolmia maritima

in America. It is a short-lived perennial usually grown as a hardy biennial for creating masses of color during late spring and early summer. The fragrant pale-blue flowers appear in open sprays, and there are varieties extending to bright-blue, indigo-blue and pink. It makes an ideal underplanting for Tulips, such as the Darwin hybrid 'Golden Apeldoorn.'

Nicotiana (Solanaceae)

The Flowering Tobacco Plant or Jasmine Tobacco (*Nicotiana alata* or *N. affinis*) is a half-hardy perennial invariably grown as a half-hardy annual, which produces clusters of long 3-inch tubular flowers in white, cream, pink, crimson, yellow or yellowish-green from early to late summer. Widely grown in the United States, this South American plant not only fills borders with color, it saturates them with a richly sweet fragrance, especially during the evening. Try growing them underneath windows so that their scent can waft indoors.

Although the leaves were once smoked and chewed by Native Americans, it is the leaves of *Nicotiana tabacum* that are widely used in the tobacco trade.

Nicotiana alata

Papaver rhoeas 'Ladybird'

Papaver (Papaveraceae)

Native to temperate "Old World" regions – and claimed to be the scourge of corn fields in Europe as well as the United States, where it became naturalized – the Corn Poppy (*Papaver rhoeas*) has been both loved and feared. In 1722, the English nurseryman Thomas Fairchild described it under the name Dutch Poppy and said it was "one of the most beautiful flowers that can be imagin'd." Few farmers at that time – and until the introduction of improved farming techniques – would have agreed with him. However, for thousands of years Corn and Poppies appear to have been inseparable.

The Assyrians knew this flower as Daughter of the Field, while later it was less flatteringly known as Canker-Rose, Devil's Tongue, Hogweed or Wartflower. It also earned the names Thunderbolt and Thundercup and Lightning because of the belief that picking it would cause a thunderstorm to occur.

In garden borders this Poppy creates a feast of 3-inch satin-red flowers with black centers from early to mid-summer. They have stiff, upright stems and plants do not require staking. Varieties of this Poppy have extended the color range to pink, rose, salmon and crimson. For a pleasing and harmonious combination, sow it amid the European Feather Grass (*Stipa pennata*), which has arching flower stems. For further interest, add the California Poppy (*Eschscholzia californica*) to this duo.

Petunia (Solanaceae)
The Petunia (*Petunia x hybridum*) is increasingly being planted in borders as well as in hanging baskets, window boxes, troughs, and other containers. It is a half-hardy perennial invariably raised as a half-hardy annual for creating a wealth of 2–4-inch-wide trumpet-shaped flowers throughout summer in colors of white,

Petunia x hybridum

Rudbeckia hirta 'Marmalade'

cream, pink, red, mauve or blue, as well as bicolored varieties. Petunias are very adaptable and can be used in several attractive combinations in borders and containers. Try a yellow-flowered Petunia in association with the blue-flowered *Salvia farinacea* and the delicate and finely-divided silvery leaves of *Tanacetum ptarmiciflorum*, earlier and still better known as *Pyrethrum ptarmiciflorum*. Try a deep purple-flowered Petunia in a container surrounded by a golden-leaved form of the trailing *Helichrysum petiolare*. This combination can also be used to great effect in hanging baskets and window boxes.

Rudbeckia (Asteraceae)
Variously known as the Coneflower, Gloriosa Daisy or Black-Eyed Susan, *Rudbeckia hirta* is a short-lived perennial invariably grown as a hardy annual. It is native to the United States where it creates a feast of bright-faced, daisy-like, 3-inch-wide flowers with yellow petals and deep brown-purple, cone-like centers from midsummer to early fall. They will self-seed freely and are happy in any soil, provided it is well drained,

Salpiglossis sinuata 'Splash'

and will flourish in either sun or shade. They are ideal for creating late color at a time when many other border plants are past their best. Remember that they are also excellent for room decoration. Incidentally, there are other glorious Coneflowers, but they have a clear and distinctive perennial nature (see page 42).

Salpiglossis (Solanaceae)

Painted Tongue (*Salpiglossis sinuata*) is another colorful annual that is widely grown in borders in the United States, where it is raised as a half-hardy annual. Sometimes it is grown in pots in greenhouses and sunrooms and taken inside as a room decoration. The funnel-shaped flowers are distinctively veined with a velvety texture. They are 2 inches long and similarly wide at their mouths. They appear in variegated shades of yellow, orange, lavender, crimson and scarlet throughout summer.

Plants have thin stems and are best supported by twiggy sticks. Insert these around plants when they are still small and you will find that stems and leaves eventually conceal them as they grow.

Salvia (Lamiaceae)

The Scarlet Sage or Bonfire Sage (*Salvia splendens*) is a stunningly attractive plant. Although a tender perennial with a shrubby habit in its native southern Brazil, it is now widely grown as a half-hardy annual in the United

Salvia splendens

States and frequently used in formal bedding displays, a way of using annuals that gained increasing popularity in the late 1800s. As its name suggests, the plant is spectacular, with scarlet flowers surrounded by similarly-colored bracts (modified petals) about 1 inch long from midsummer to the onset of cold weather. It can now be seen in other colors, including purple, salmon and white, and is often used in conjunction with white Alyssum, Lobelia, and small Marigolds in formal displays. It is sometimes grown as a potted plant for room decoration.

Tagetes (Asteraceae)

Mexico is the home of many colorful annuals and few are better known than the Big Marigold or Aztec Marigold (*Tagetes erecta*), which is better but rather misleadingly known as the African Marigold. When seeds were taken to Spain in the sixteenth century it was widely known as the "Rose of the Indies." It became naturalized on the Algerian coast of North Africa and by the mid-sixteenth century was assumed to be an African native. It was reintroduced into Europe under the name *Flos africanus* and was known as the Common Africane, and later as the African Marigold.

The large daisy-like, 2-inch lemon-yellow flowers appear from midsummer to the frosts of early fall. This dramatic annual can be a difficult neighbor for other bedding plants because of its dominating color. Try it on its own in large drifts, or as a filler for bare areas in newly-planted mixed borders. It can also be planted in containers on patios.

Its near-relative, *Tagetes patula*, is another Mexican beauty and widely known as the French Marigold.

Tagates patula

Trachymene coerulea

Trachymene (Apiaceae)
The Blue Lace Flower (*Trachymene coerulea*), otherwise known as *Didiscus coerulea*, is a Western Australian summer-flowering annual with lightly-scented, slightly domed, lavender-blue flowers. Sow it in a large group towards the front of an annual border so that the delicately-colored flowers can be fully appreciated. It is useful as a cut flower and is particularly attractive in mixed bouquets. In the garden, take care not to position it with strongly-colored flowers close by as this will greatly detract from its ethereal beauty.

Tropaeolum (Tropaeolaceae)
Commonly known as the Nasturtium, Garden Nasturtium, Mexican Cress or Indian Cress, Tropaeolums are popular natives from Mexico to Central America, Argentina and Peru. There are many types, including annuals and herbaceous perennials, some with a climbing habit. Perhaps the best known of these is *Tropaeolum majus*, an annual which climbs and trails and has distinctive circular, mid-green leaves with wavy edges. From early summer to fall it reveals faintly sweet-smelling flowers. Originally these were yellow or orange, but red, pink, salmon and maroon forms are now available.

Tall and vigorous varieties are useful for climbing screens or for sprawling over banks, while dwarf types are ideal for planting in window boxes and hanging baskets.

When crushed, the leaves have a pungent aroma and their use is recorded in Turkish cookbooks. Dwight D. Eisenhower, the 34th President of the United States, is said to have used Nasturtiums in his recipe for vegetable soup, while the flower buds and seeds are used as a substitute for capers and to flavor vinegar.

There are many other Tropaeolums: the Peruvian and Bolivian *Tropaeolum tuberosum*, known locally as *anyu*, is a vigorous climber up to 10-feet-high, with lobed leaves and red-and-yellow flowers during the early fall. More attractive, however, is the perennial Chilean Flame Creeper (*T. speciosum*), with brilliant scarlet flowers, and the popular Peruvian Canary Creeper (*T. peregrinum*), but earlier known as *T. canariense*, with irregularly-shaped yellow flowers. Both plants have a climbing and twining habit and will create magnificent displays in your garden. The Chilean Flame Creeper looks good scrambling over shrubs.

Zinnia (Asteraceae)

The Common Zinnia or Youth and Age (*Zinnia elegans*) is a half-hardy annual that produces a mass of bright purple flowers, each up to 2 inches across, from

Zinnia elegans

midsummer to the frosts of early fall. There are many varieties which come in a range of white, purple, yellow, orange, red and pink. As well as decorating annual borders and filling spaces in mixed borders, try planting low-growing varieties in window boxes and other containers on a patio. Don't forget to pinch out the growing tips of the young plants to encourage bushiness.

Although it did not arrive in Europe until 1796, the Zinnia was abundant in Montezuma's Mexican gardens some 200 years or more earlier, where it grew alongside Dahlias, Sunflowers, Tigridias (Tiger Flowers) and Convolvulus; this created a far greater spectacle than any display seen in Europe at that time.

Tropaeolum majus

Handsome Perennials

America is particularly fortunate in her hardy herbaceous perennials which create a dramatic display during summer each year. In the fall, the onset of cold weather destroys the leaves and stems but in spring the dormant roots send up fresh shoots and the process begins again. These plants are ideal in beds totally devoted to herbaceous perennials, or in "mixed" borders planted with a range of other plants, from bulbs to shrubs and an occasional tree. Perennials are robust and resilient and need little attention. Some, however, will benefit from a little support, especially in exposed areas. Insert twiggy sticks while the plants are still young. These will cease to be noticeable as the plant matures.

Alchemilla (Rosaceae)

The incomparable Lady's Mantle (*Alchemilla mollis*) is ideal for planting in beds alongside pathways, where it will help soften harsh edges. It has rounded, shallowly-lobed and serrated, hairy, light-green leaves and masses of tiny, sulfur-yellow flowers borne in loose sprays throughout summer. In borders it is a superb companion to roses, where it helps to cloak bare stems. As well as decorating borders, the leaves and stems are ideal for adding to floral arrangements to be displayed indoors.

Allium moly

Alchemilla mollis

Alchemilla vulgaris is a similar species and has the same common name, as well as being called Lion's Foot, Duck's Foot or Dew-Cup, which refers to the attractive way the plant collects pearls of dew in its leaves. It is said to have magical qualities, and in the sixteenth century was used to heal wounds and stop bleeding.

Allium (Alliaceae)

Most perennial borders are eclectic, with plants native to many countries, including America. Southern Europe has given us the unforgettable Golden Leek (*Allium moly*), which is popularly known as Golden Garlic, the Lily Leek or Yellow Onion. It is hardy and herbaceous and creates a mass of bright-yellow, star-shaped flowers in small umbrella-like clusters during early and mid-summer. Its greyish-green leaves are strap-like and when encircled by the silvery-leaved *Lamium maculatum* 'Beacon Silver,' the whole plant is attractively highlighted.

Anaphalis (Asteraceae)
With an American and East Asian heritage, the Pearl Everlasting (*Anaphalis margaritacea*) is at home in herbaceous borders on many continents. It is known for its grey-green tapering leaves and heads of pearly-white flowers during late summer. If you are considering creating a grey-leaved border, this plant is essential. Additionally, the flower heads can be used fresh or dried in floral arrangements for indoor decoration.

Earlier known as *A. yedoensis*, but now correctly as *A. margaritacea yedoensis*, this Japanese plant is popular in the United States and has white, closely-bunched flower heads from midsummer to fall. A few other related plants are popular in herbaceous borders and these include the Himalayan *A. triplinervis* with silver-grey leaves covered with small, woolly hairs; these have the bonus of white flowers borne in bunched heads which appear in late summer.

Anaphalis triplinervis

Anemone x hybrida

Anemone (Ranunculaceae)
The Japanese Anemone or Japanese Windflower (*Anemone x hybrida*) encompasses a wide range of hardy herbaceous perennials that, like Sedum 'Autumn Joy,' are glorious in the fall. It develops upright stems bearing white to deep-rose saucer-shaped flowers, each about 3 inches wide. It is ideal for mingling with tall rose bushes, or in a large drift in a bed or under a deciduous tree.

Aster sedifolius (acris)

Aster (Asteraceae)
The southern European *Aster sedifolius*, still better known as *A. acris*, has a bushy habit and creates a distinctive massed display of 1-inch lavender-blue, daisy-like flowers with golden centers during late summer and fall. Like many blue-flowered plants, it is ideal for positioning close to neighbors with soft yellow flowers or light-green leaves, such as Lady's Mantle (*Alchemilla mollis*).

Astilbe (Saxifragaceae)
Often known as perennial Spiraeas, these herbaceous plants have a hardy habit and are ideal for borders as well as alongside streams and garden ponds. *Astilbe x arendsii* has dark-green, fern-like leaves and masses of pyramidal, feather-like flower heads from early to late summer. There are many varieties, including 'Amethyst' (lilac-rose), 'Bressingham Beauty' (pink), 'Fanal' (dark-red) and 'White Glory' (white), now properly known as 'Weisse Gloria.'

Large drifts of Astilbes in moisture-retentive soil sloping down to a pond look superb, especially if seen from a slightly higher vantage point, while in borders they make ideal companions for Hemerocallis and large Candelabra Primulas.

Astilbe x arendsii

Camassia quamash (esculenta)

Camassia (Hyacinthacaea)
Camass, Qamash or Comosh (*Camassia quamash*) is a bulbous-based hardy perennial. Also known as *C. esculenta*, it comes from western states and has long, narrow leaves and upright stems that bear clusters of star-like flowers in white, blue or purple from late spring to mid-summer. For a spectacular display, plant a vivid orange variety of the Siberian Wallflower around blue-flowered clumps of Camassia.

The bulbs, which are low in starch and high in sugar, were once gathered by Native Americans and early settlers for their food value, roasted on hot stones, and dried and stored for use during winter. Another common name is Bear Grass, which indicates the liking bears are said to have for the plant.

Coreopsis (Asteraceae)
The perennial Tickseed (*Coreopsis verticillata*), an American native, is a popular part of many herbaceous borders, creating a mass of bright-green, somewhat fern-like leaves and clear-yellow 1-inch flowers throughout summer. There are several superb varieties, including 'Grandiflora' (also known as 'Golden Shower') with rich yellow flowers, and 'Zagreb' with

Coreopsis verticillata

golden-yellow flowers on shorter plants. It is an ideal plant for a mixed border, where it produces a long-lasting display of color with a clear and distinctive outline.

This Tickseed, together with the annual *C. tinctoria* (page 53), was used to dye cloth red by the Native Americans.

Crocosmia (Iridaceae)
Popularly known as Montbretia or Falling Stars, *Crocosmia x crocosmiiflora*, earlier known as *Montbretia crocosmiiflora*, is a slightly tender cormous plant with a clump-forming habit and narrow, arching, sword-like leaves. Funnel-shaped flowers appear from mid- to late summer in shades ranging from yellow to deep red. Plants spread rapidly and usually need to be divided and replanted every three years. For an unusual combination of plants, position the variegated Prairie Cord Grass (*Spartina pectinata* 'Aureomarginata') behind *Crocosmia x crocosmiiflora* 'Solfatare,' with apricot-yellow flowers and bronze-flushed leaves.

Delphinium (Ranunculaceae)
Few plants are as distinctive as the Delphinium, and especially *Delphinium elatum*, an herbaceous perennial native to a wide area from south and central Europe to Siberia. The first specimens introduced into cultivation came from Siberia in 1597; they bore a resemblance to present-day plants but had smaller flowers. Nowadays, the true species is seldom grown and it is a group of hybrids that decorate gardens and have become widely cultivated in the United States.

There are two distinct forms of these plants: Elatum types have tall, erect stems packed with large florets mainly in shades of blue but also mauve, lavender and white during early and mid-summer, in single, semi-double and double forms. The Belladonnas are of unknown origin but named forms were raised from 1890 onwards. They are graceful and branching. No country house garden should be without them, their loose spikes of florets in pale-blue, gentian-blue, violet-blue, pink or white swaying gently in the wind.

Crocosmia x crocosmiiflora

Delphinium elatum

Dicentra spectabilis

The Elatum types create dramatic features in herbaceous borders. A combination of a dominant blue variety as a backcloth for a lighter blue-flowered *Campanula lactiflora* and white Madonna Lily (*Lilium candidum*) is superb. For added interest, plant the half-hardy annual *Nicotiana alata* 'Lime Green' at the border's front, and the tall and yellow-flowered *Thalictrum speciosissimum* behind the Delphinium. (You might now find the Thalictrum listed in some catalogs as *T. flavum glaucum.*)

Dicentra (Papaveraceae)
Dicentras have both an American and Asian heritage, *Dicentra spectabilis* from Siberia and northern China being the preferred species. *D. canadensis*, the Squirrel Corn, also known as the Turkey Pea, comes from Canada and parts of the United States. In spring it bears white flowers tinged with mauve.

Dicentra formosa is another American plant, with a delicate appearance but resilient nature. It develops fern-like, bright-green leaves and pink, narrow heart-shaped flowers in arching clusters during late spring and early summer. Try planting it in gaps in an old stone wall. Alternatively, plant it near the front of a border, but do not crowd it with other plants.

Other popular American species include Golden Eardrops (*D. chrysantha*) from southern California, Dutchman's Breeches (*D. cucullaria*), North Carolina and west to Kansas, and the Turkey Corn or Staggerweed (*D. eximia*).

Dictamnus (Rutaceae)
Popular names can be misleading, especially when they refer to two different plants. The half-hardy annual *Kochia scoparia* 'Trichophylla' is grown for its light-green foliage that turns deep red in the fall and has therefore given rise to the popular and descriptive name Burning Bush, but to many gardeners it is the

herbaceous *Dictamnus albus*, earlier and still widely known as *D. fraxinella*, to which this common name belongs. It comes from southern Europe and Asia and is also known as Fraxinella, Dittany, Bastard Dittany, False Dittany, White Dittany or Gas Plant. The plant develops upright spires of fragrant, spider-like white flowers during early and mid-summer. The variety 'Purpureus' has pink flowers with red stripes.

For many years this striking plant has produced a theatrical effect in borders; it is strongly aromatic and the seed heads are especially rich in oils. During warm, still summer evenings it sometimes creates a halo of volatilized oil that can be ignited. In borders the variety 'Purpureus' is a superb companion for a light-blue Cranesbill (Geranium) and the

Dictamnus albus

Dodecatheon media

Golden-Leaved Sage (*Salvia officinalis* 'Icterina').

Fraxinella is also famed for its medicinal qualities; the root coatings are claimed to ease fevers, while an infusion of the leaves makes a tea supposedly useful for nervous complaints.

Dodecatheon (Primulaceae)

Widely known as the American Cowslip or Shooting Stars, *Dodecatheon media* is native to a large part of America, where it creates a distinctive display. Plants have light-green, oval to oblong leaves and stems bearing rose-purple flowers with bright-yellow anthers during late spring and early summer. The flowers are distinctive and very attractive, therefore it is preferable not to crowd them with other plants. Dodecatheons are claimed to be the primulas of the New World.

Dodecatheons thrive in light shade and moist, leafy soil, so plant them in a woodland setting where they can be left undisturbed to form large clumps.

Erigeron speciosus

Erigeron (Asteraceae)

The Fleabanes were once considered to be less attractive than their near relatives, the Asters, because they had only a single row of ray-florets in contrast to the two of the Aster. However, few gardeners could fail to be captivated by the Oregon Fleabane (*Erigeron speciosus*), native to the western states and a plant with masses of daisy-like purple flowers which appear throughout summer.

There are many varieties, including 'Charity' (clear-pink), 'Darkest of All' (deep violet-blue), 'Dignity' (violet-blue), 'Foerster's Liebling' (deep-pink), 'Quakeress' (light mauve-pink), and 'Schwarzes Meer' (lavender-violet with yellow centers). Plants are best seen in large groups; take care not to position dominant bright-yellow plants too close to them.

Stories of how Erigerons got their common name are legion: the English gardener and herbalist John Parkinson claimed that Fleabane, when bound to the forehead, helped cure the "frensie," while during the 1600s the apothecary and astrologer-physician Nicholas Culpeper reported that Fleabane was so named because its seeds were said to resemble fleas.

Erythronium (Liliaceae)

Popularly known as the American Trout Lily or American Adder's Tongue, the bulbous-rooted *Erythronium revolutum* is native across much of the United States. Its green leaves are lightly mottled white and brown, while the nodding, six-petaled, Turk's-Cap-like flowers appear in spring in a wide color range from near-white to pink or purple, and with darker mottling.

For a white-and-blue color combination, plant *Erythronium revolutum* 'White Beauty' amid the soft blue *Anemone nemorosa* 'Allenii,' a Wood Anemone. Alternatively, plant a ring of the American Trout Lily

Erythronium revolutum

Filipendula purpurea

around the base of a deciduous tree, where they can flourish in the light shade.

Several other Erythroniums are native to the United States, including *E. americanum*, the Yellow Adder's Tongue, Amberbell or Serpent's Tongue from the eastern states. *E. tuolumnense*, the Fawn Lily, is native to California. The Dog's-Tooth Violet (*E. dens-canis*), however, is European and Asian, with pink-purple flowers and green leaves blotched brown or grey.

Light shade and fertile, moisture-retentive soil suit all of these Erythroniums and they can be grown with many other plants, including Dodecatheons.

Filipendula (Rosaceae)

We now know the herbaceous Spiraeas as Filipendulas rather than Spiraeas, and many of them adorn borders where they create a reliable display year upon year. One of the most spectacular is *Filipendula purpurea*, popularly known as Meadowsweet and earlier as *Spiraea palmata.* During midsummer this hardy plant creates masses of large, fluffy heads composed of carmine to pink flowers, which are borne among deeply-cut, green leaves. It is ideal for planting in formal herbaceous borders as well as in country gardens, where it has a relaxed and informal appeal.

The Meadowsweet or Queen of the Meadows (*Filipendula ulmaria*) is native to Europe and north and central Asia, and is now widely naturalized in the United States. With small creamy-white flowers borne in flattened heads up to 6 inches wide throughout summer, it is an asset to any border. It is steeped in history: apart from its use in earlier times for strewing the floors of halls and banqueting-houses, when it produced an almond-like fragrance, it was one of the 50 ingredients in a substance called "Save," which was mentioned by the English poet Geoffrey Chaucer in the Knight's Tale from *The Canterbury Tales*, written towards the end of the 1300s.

Geranium endressii

The Queen of the Prairies (*Filipendula rubra*) is an all-American border plant and a native of the eastern states. It develops deep-pink or peach-pink flowers on branching stems during mid- and late summer. Like all other Filipendulas, it creates a dramatic feature in herbaceous borders as well as proving its worth in mixed borders where it will grow happily amid shrubs and other herbaceous plants.

Geranium (Geraniaceae)

The Geranium or Cranesbill family is an eclectic group of plants found in many temperate regions. *Geranium maculatum*, an American native, bears light- to deep-magenta-pink flowers and is known as Wild Geranium or Wild Cranesbill. Another name is Alumroot, a reference to the fact that dried roots were once used to treat a wide range of medical problems, including dysentery and internal bleeding.

Geranium endressii is often seen in borders, where it creates a mass of pale-pink flowers lightly veined with red. It is a resilient plant and ideal for creating ground cover over a large area where conditions are dry, in either light shade or full sun.

The Meadow Cranesbill (*G. pratense*), a European native widely grown in America, produces a feast of blue or violet-blue flowers with crimson veins during mid- and late summer. There are several superb varieties in white and shades of blue, some with double flowers. Again, plants have a tolerance of near-drought conditions yet bravely create magnificent displays.

Gypsophila (Caryophyllaceae)

Baby's Breath (*Gypsophila paniculata*), also known as the Chalk Plant or Gauze Plant, is a widely-grown border plant from southern Europe, the Caucasus and Siberia. It has finely-divided stems bearing a mass of small, usually white flowers during early and mid-summer. There are several superb varieties, including

Gypsophila paniculata

'Bristol Fairy' (double and bright-white), 'Flamingo' (double and pale-pink) and 'Compacta Plena' (double and white).

Take care not to position these plants too close to color-dominant flowers such as those with dramatic yellow or strong red flowers. However, plants with soft yellow flowers make ideal bedfellows. Gypsophila is frequently used in bouquets and other flower arrangements where it creates an attractive background to showier flowers.

Helenium (Asteraceae)

The Sneezeweed (*Helenium autumnale*), a hardy, fibrous-rooted plant from parts of the United States and Canada, creates a mass of 1-inch daisy-like yellow flowers from midsummer to the fall on plants up to 6 feet high. The center of each flower forms a dominant cone. Varieties extend the color range to orange, copper, bronze-red and crimson-mahogany and enable a wide variety of combinations to be created. For example, a bronze-red variety of this Sneezeweed and a backing of yellow Helianthus looks superb. For a further enhancement, add a dark-red Crocosmia to one side. For a dramatic display in a mixed border, try a dominant patch of a yellow variety of Sneezeweed.

Helenium autumnale

Hemerocallis 'Pink Damask'

Hemerocallis (Hemerocallidaceae)
The spectacular Day Lilies, native to Eastern Asia, Japan and China, were known to the Greek army doctor Dioscorides in the first century AD for their medicinal qualities. Moreover, when dried, the flowers of *Hemerocallis fulva* were used as a condiment in China and Japan. Together with *H. flava*, the Lemon Lily, it had arrived in England by the end of the 1500s and soon after appeared in America. In the United States *H. fulva* became known as the Orange Day Lily or Fulvous Day Lily as well as the Tawny Day Lily.

American gardeners have taken to Day Lilies with great enthusiasm, not least because it is a plant that can be successfully grown in a wide range of soils, from sand to clay. Nowadays, it is mainly the garden hybrids that are grown, in colors such as ruby-purple, golden-yellow, maroon-red, pink and brick-red.

The Hemerocallis, with its upright nature and strongly-colored flowers, can be used to create sudden variations in height as well as dramatic bursts of color. For example, a yellow-flowered Hemerocallis is ideal for positioning next to Geranium 'Johnson's Blue,' a robust herbaceous perennial.

Hosta (Hostaceae)
Hostas, previously botanically known as Funkias and popularly in America as Plantain Lilies, are grown for their attractive leaves and nodding, trumpet-like flowers. *Hosta fortunei* 'Albopicta' has pale-green leaves with buff-yellow variegations on plants 18–20 inches high. During midsummer it bears 1-inch-long lilac flowers. Other Hostas are taller and more dominant, including 'Tall Boy,' with spires of violet-mauve flowers on plants of up to 3 feet high. As well as planting them alongside paths and with other plants in borders, relatively low-growing and bushy Hostas are ideal for planting in large containers positioned on a patio or wide path. As well as making the Hostas easy to see, this is also useful for helping to prevent slugs from eating the leaves, especially during wet and warm summers.

Kniphofia (Asphodelaceae)
There are many perennials now grown mainly in their hybrid forms and these include the spectacular Kniphofias, popularly known as Torch Lilies, Poker Plants or Red-Hot Pokers. Native to South Africa, they grow outdoors in the northern hemisphere but

Hosta fortunei 'Albopicta'

Kniphofia 'Enchantress'

welcome protection of their roots in cold areas; a layer of straw 4–6 inches thick will protect their crowns. The flower heads are poker-like, in shades of yellow, lemon-yellow, flame-orange, bright scarlet-red or orange-red.

Like the Hemerocallis, Kniphofias make a dominant feature in borders and are especially attractive when seen against clear blue skies.

Limonium (Plumbaginaceae)

A hardy perennial with a woody rootstock, *Limonium platyphyllum*, still better known as *Limonium latifolium* and *Statice limonium*, is native to a wide area of southeast and central Europe and is popularly known as Sea Lavender. In borders it creates lavender-blue flowers in clusters of up to 9 inches from midsummer to fall, amid rosettes of green downy leaves. There are several superb varieties, including 'Violetta' with violet flowers.

Position this plant towards the front of a border; the stems and flowers often lean over the edges of beds and onto pathways, where they help to soften harsh lines. However, the grass may be damaged if the border is edged by a lawn.

The Marsh Rosemary or Sea Lavender (*Limonium carolinianum*), a related species native to salt marshes on the east coast, has lavender-colored flowers and roots which have been used medicinally in the treatment of diarrhea and dysentery, and as a gargling and mouthwash for easing mouth ulcers, catarrh and sore throats.

Lupinus (Paplionaceae)

Some Lupins have American ancestry, including *Lupinus polyphyllus*, a native of the area stretching from California to British Columbia and the main parent of the world-famous Russell Lupins, which were developed by the British gardener George Russell.

In its wild form, this Lupin has purple-blue flowers, but white, pale-pink and bicolored forms are occasionally seen. The improvement of the species began in the early 1900s when it was crossed with *L. arboreus*, another North American species. This is the

Limonium platyphyllum (latifolium)

Lupinus arboreus

yellow-flowered and sweetly honey-scented Tree Lupin from California. This crossing initially introduced yellow and subsequently rich crimson to the plants. Other species are claimed to be in the ancestry of Russell Lupins, including the California to Washington *L. laxiflorus*. Nowadays, border forms have flowers in red, deep-pink, orange and yellow, as well as bicolored types in purple and gold, pink and amethyst, apricot and blue, and many others. Few borders are complete without these glorious, dramatic and distinctive flowers. A border packed with mixed-color Russell Lupins is certain to attract attention, but remember to cut off the flowering stems after the flowers fade to prevent the development of self-sown seedlings. This will often encourage a further flush of flowers.

Lysichiton (Araceae)

Together with the Kamchatka peninsula, an area in northeast Russia, the United States and Canada have two of the "stinkers" of the plant world. *Lysichiton americanus*, the Skunk Cabbage, Yellow Skunk Cabbage or Western Skunk Cabbage, produces deep golden-yellow, Arum-like flowers during spring. These have a very disagreeable aroma which is said to be a combination of skunk, carrion and garlic. The smell attracts flies and midges in such great numbers that spiders weave webs between and on the plants to trap them for food. Despite the appalling smell of the flowers, the roots were eaten as a vegetable by Native Americans. The roots are said to have medicinal properties for purifying the blood. The leaves have also been used to make poultices.

L. camtschatcensis is similar but slightly smaller, having white, Arum-like flowers which reveal an unpleasant animal-like odor. Both of these plants are ideal for planting in wet soil alongside natural ponds or at the margins of bog gardens.

Meconopsis (Papaveraceae)

There are some plants that immediately command attention, and the Blue Poppy or Himalayan Blue Poppy (*Meconopsis betonicifolia*) is one of these. It has a hardy and herbaceous habit and produces oblong, mid-green leaves with clear sky-blue flowers, each up to 3 inches wide during early and mid-summer. The intense blue flowers are unforgettable, and when planted in large groups in fertile, moisture-retentive soil in light shade it is superb. Alternatively, try it behind a clump of *Hosta fortunei* 'Albopicta,' with variegated leaves and lilac-coloured flowers during midsummer, and with a backcloth of the Honeysuckle *Lonicera x tellmanniana*, which twines around supports and grows to 10 feet or more. It bears masses of red and yellow flowers during early and mid-summer.

Lysichiton americanus

Meconopsis betonicifolia

Monarda (Lamiaceae)
Monarda didyma is a popular herbaceous perennial widely known as Oswego Tea, Bee Balm or Sweet Bergamot. Native to the United States and Canada, it creates masses of scarlet, up to 3-inch-wide whorled heads throughout summer. In addition, there are varieties with bright-scarlet, pink, violet-purple, bright-red and white flowers. The bright-red varieties create a dramatic and dominant display and are best used in small groups, while white and pink forms can be used in larger blocks. For a delicate arrangement, try the pink-flowered 'Croftway Pink' against a pale-red Dahlia.

Monardas yield an essential oil used in perfumery and as a hair tonic. Native Americans once used the leaves as a vegetable and to create a refreshing tea.

Monarda didyma

Perovskia atriplicifolia

Perovskia (Lamiaceae)
Although it has a shrubby and semi-woody habit, the Russian Sage (*Perovskia atriplicifolia*) is invariably grown in herbaceous borders. This is because in late fall or winter all stems are cut down to 1–1½ foot above ground level to encourage the development in spring and summer of a feast of long, stiffly-erect stems that bear coarsely-toothed, grey-green leaves with a sage-like odor. During late summer and into fall it bears an abundance of violet-blue flowers.

Both the flowers and leaves create a delicate feature in borders, so take care not to position color-dominant plants near them. Soft, primrose-yellow and lemon flowers harmonize well with Russian Sage.

Phlox (Polemoniaceae)
The Phlox family has an American and Mexican ancestry. Few border plants are more attractive than *Phlox paniculata*, widely known as the Fall Phlox, Perennial Phlox or Fall-flowering Phlox. It has large heads of sweetly-scented 1-inch-wide flowers from midsummer to early fall. There are many varieties, with white, salmon-orange, scarlet, salmon-pink, claret-red and pink flowers. Older clumps are usually divided in fall and the woody inner parts discarded before replanting.

Phlox paniculata 'Eventide'

Rudbeckia fulgida 'Goldsturm'

Rudbeckia (Asteraceae)

The Coneflower (*Rudbeckia laciniata*), another superb American plant, has oval, mid-green leaves and 3–4-inch-wide yellow flowers during late summer and into the fall. *Rudbeckia fulgida* from the southeastern states is also spectacular. Earlier known as *R. speciosa*, it creates a feast of yellow to orange daisy-like flowers, each about 2 inches wide, and with a large, purple-brown cone-like center. There are several superb varieties, including 'Speciosa' (orange), 'Goldsturm' (yellow) and 'Deamii' (also yellow). These yellow-flowered plants are ideal for introducing a vibrant accent to a garden. Remember also that yellow-flowered plants remain noticeable until late in the evening, long after purple and dark-red flowers have merged into the darkness.

A similar American herbaceous perennial was first classified as *Rudbeckia purpurea*, but later named *Echinacea purpurea*. It is another plant whose flowers have cone-like centers. However, the 4-inch-wide flowers are not yellow but a rich purple-crimson with an orange center. There are many varieties, including

Few plants have such deliciously fragrant flowers, most noticeable in the evening. For a superb display in late summer, try planting *Rosa rugosa* 'Roseraie de l'Haÿ' with crimson flowers as a background and the pink-flowered *Phlox paniculata* 'Eventide' in front of it. The silver-leaved *Santolina chamaecyparissus* could also be positioned nearby.

The Wild Sweet William (*Phlox maculata*), from the eastern states, has even more fragrant flowers, borne in tapering heads up to 6 inches long. They are normally purple, but pure white and pink varieties are available. When positioning these flowers in a border, try putting them near the front so that their fragrance can be fully appreciated.

Few medicinal qualities are attributed to Phloxes, but the False Pinkroot (*P. carolina*), also known as the Thick-Leaf Phlox, has sometimes been confused with *Spigelia marilandica*, an American native widely known as Pink Root, Star-Bloom, Indian Pink, Maryland Pinkroot or Worm Grass. It is this last popular name that indicates its medicinal use; the dried rhizomes were used to treat intestinal worms. Its value as a vermifuge was well known to Native Americans, especially members of the Cherokee and Creek tribes, who collected the roots to sell to white traders.

Smilacina racemosa

Sedum 'Herbstfreude' ('Autumn Joy')

'Robert Bloom' (purple-rose) and 'White Luster' (white). It is popularly known as the Purple Coneflower and Black Sampson. Although individual flowers are dramatic and attractive, the plants do not have as many flowers as the yellow Rudbeckias.

Sedum (Crassulaceae)

Sedum 'Autumn Joy,' as its name suggests, is spectacular in the fall. Earlier known as *Sedum spectabile* 'Autumn Joy' and now properly as Sedum 'Herbstfreude' and popularly as Giant Stonecrop or Ice Plant, it is a hardy border perennial with pale-green, glossy and somewhat pear-shaped, fleshy leaves. During late summer it produces 4–8-inch slightly dome-shaped heads of salmon-pink flowers that slowly change through orange-red to orange-brown by mid- to late fall.

For a pleasing combination, plant a clump of Sedum 'Autumn Joy' with a frill of the mauve Lilyturf (*Lirope muscari*). To the sides of the Sedum, position the blue-flowered Chinese Plumbago (*Ceratostigma willmottianum*) and yellow-flowered Goldenrod (Solidago).

Smilacina (Convallariaceae)

Also known as False Spikenard, False Solomon's Seal, Zig-Zag or Solomon's Plumes, *Smilacina racemosa*, is an American native, where it delights in moist, fertile soil and light shade. During late spring and early summer it produces arching, terminal flower sprays of creamy-white, sweetly-scented flowers. The plants have a relaxed, informal habit making them ideally suited to the mixed border or a country garden ambience. Later,

Solidago 'Crown of Rays'

plants develop green then red berries, sometimes mottled red or purple, that were eaten by Native Americans in Oregon and British Columbia. Early settlers knew them as Scurvy Berries as they contain a large amount of vitamin C. The leaves of plants were used by Native Americans in Nevada to make a drink said to act as a contraceptive, while members of the Blackfoot tribe utilized powdered roots to treat wounds.

The Star-Flowered Lily-of-the-Valley (*Smilacina stellata*) reveals arching stems that bear sprays of sweetly-scented, white star-shaped flowers during late spring and early summer. Again, this is a relaxed and informal plant and best grown in a country-style garden.

Solidago (Asteraceae)

Mainly herbaceous perennials from the United States, Solidagos bear masses of tiny yellow flowers in plume-like heads. Although several species are grown, it is mainly the hybrids that adorn gardens. These have been developed from the Canada Goldenrod (*Solidago canadensis*) and the European *Solidago virgaurea*, also known as the Common Goldenrod. Varieties include the well-known 'Crown of Rays' (bright-yellow), 'Goldenmosa' (yellow-green foliage and yellow flowers) and 'Queenie' (earlier known as 'Golden Thumb'), with golden-yellow flowers on plants only 1 foot high.

For a delicate and refined display, position Solidago 'Goldenmosa' next to the white-flowered Obedient Plant *Physostegia virginiana* 'Summer Snow.' (Incidentally, 'Goldenmosa' gained its name from the resemblance of the flowers to Mimosa.)

The Canadian Goldenrod, also known as Gerbe d'Or, has seeds that were eaten by Native Americans, while the European Goldenrod, additionally known as Verge d'Or, Woundworth, Aaron's Rod or Goldruthe, has roots and leaves used medicinally as a mild sedative and to treat digestive upsets; the leaves were also used as a poultice to draw wounds.

Tradescantia (Commelinaceae)

Popularly known in America as the Spiderwort or Widow's Tears, *Tradescantia virginiana* is also called the Trinity Flower because each flower has three petals which has given it a religious significance; Moses in the Bulrushes is yet another name. It was given the name Spiderwort through its initial erroneous classification as a "phalangium," a cure for the bite of the phalangium spider, later established as quite harmless.

It is a distinctive plant, with long, narrow, sword-like green leaves and striking violet-purple flowers. Nowadays, there are several superb varieties and perhaps one of the best is 'Isis,' with rich royal-purple flowers from early to late summer. There are other varieties and these include 'Purple Dome' (rich purple) and 'Osprey' (white).

As if being decorative were not enough, it is said that young shoots and leaves were occasionally used in salads and as a vegetable in early times in America.

For a blue display, plant a blue-flowered Tradescantia towards the front of a border, with a backing of the hardy herbaceous *Campanula lactiflora* 'Pritchard's Variety.'

Tradescantia 'Isis'

Inspiring Indoor Flower Displays

Flower arranging has always been popular and is a relatively inexpensive way to add a personal touch to your home. Florist's flowers, such as Chrysanthemums and Carnations, are always available, but don't forget the humbler flowers, sometimes ignored, and which you can grow yourself. Here are a slew of ideas to brighten your home and your life.

Chrysanthemum (Asteraceae)

The Chrysanthemum has been cultivated in China for more than 2,500 years and was a favorite flower of the Mandarins. It became both a garden and enthusiast's flower, but it is mainly to American and English plant scientists in the 1950s that we owe the modern Chrysanthemum which is commercially grown for

Chrysanthemum carinatum

Chrysanthemum 'Elworthy'

Dianthus caryophyllus

cutting. It was discovered that by controlling the temperature and the comparative length of light and darkness in greenhouses, flowers could be obtained throughout the year. Technically, Chrysanthemums are known as "short-day" plants as they normally start to produce flower buds when the amount of daylight is less than the dark in a period of 24 hours. They became known as "all-year-round" Chrysanthemums and have the bonus of lasting several weeks when cut and displayed indoors. They are also commercially grown in pots: these are ideal for offices as they survive with little attention.

Dianthus (Caryophyllaceae)

The Dianthus or Carnation is now an indispensable feature of gardens and greenhouses. The early development of perpetual-flowering Carnations took place in Lyon, France, in 1830, and continued there for many years. In the 1860s and 70s, American breeders imported seeds and plants from France and continued their own breeding programs, while towards the end of that century nurserymen began the practice of disbudding Carnations to create larger and more distinctive flowers. This continues to this day, although some nurseries take the cheaper option and leave them as sprays, each stem bearing many but smaller flowers.

Gladiolus (Iridaceae)

These cormous plants are wonderful for creating extravagant displays indoors as well as in gardens. The large-flowered hybrids are most popular, with strong and erect stems of up to 20 inches packed with colorful florets from the latter part of summer to the early fall. Their range is wide and includes golden-yellow, salmon-orange, deep violet-blue, orange-scarlet, violet-purple, silvery-white and greenish-lemon.

For room decoration, cut the spikes when the lowest floret is just opening. Use a sharp knife or pruning shears to sever each stem with a slanted cut, leaving at least four leaves on the cut stump to enable the corm to continue growing healthily. Plunge the cut stems

Gladiolus 'Spic and Span'

Floribunda Rose 'Strawberry Ice'

immediately into deep water in a cool room for about a day. They are then ready to be arranged in vases.

Rosa (Rosaceae)

Roses create magnificent displays in gardens as well as in indoor arrangements. The most popular roses for home decoration are the Hybrid Teas (large-flowered bush), with long stems, exquisitely-shaped flowers and often with the bonus of a rich fragrance. Floribundas (cluster-flowered bush) are another popular type for cutting, their flowers borne in large clusters which seem to arrange themselves.

Although Roses do not always last as long in water as Chrysanthemums or Carnations, they create such romantic displays in a wide range of both rich and subtle colors that they are often the first choice. There are, of course, ways of extending their lives and these include cutting stems early in the morning when they are full of moisture and standing them in deep water in a cool, dark basement for 24 hours before arranging them. Removing the lower leaves and slitting the base of each stem for about an inch also helps to prolong their life. Cut Hybrid Tea varieties when the sepals (green parts around the base of each flower) have opened and the petals are in bud and beginning to show color. In the case of Floribundas, most of the

Hybrid Tea Rose 'Troika'

flowers in the truss should ideally be half-open.

Many Hybrid Tea varieties are ideal for both garden and home display and these include 'Alexander' (orange-vermilion and slightly fragrant), 'Blue Moon' (silvery-lilac and very fragrant), 'Ophelia' (pale-pink with a yellow base and very fragrant) and 'Troika' (orange-bronze, shaded red and fragrant).

Suitable Floribundas include 'Anne Harkness' (apricot-yellow and slightly fragrant), 'Margaret Merril' (pearly-white and very fragrant), 'Pink Parfait' (pink with a cream base), 'Queen Elizabeth' (light-pink and slightly fragrant) and 'Redgold' (golden-yellow, edged with cherry-red and slightly fragrant).

Consider Roses with attractive leaves as well as beautiful flowers. Leaves add a long-lasting quality to a display as well as creating a feature that is sure to earn admiration. Suitable varieties include *Rosa glauca* (earlier and still better known as *R. rubrifolia*), with glaucous-purple stems adorned with grey-purple leaves, *R.* 'Roseraie de l'Haÿ,' a rugosa type with bright, leathery, wrinkled green leaves, and *Rosa xanthina* 'Canary Bird' with graceful, bright-green, fern-like leaves.

Rosa 'Margaret Merril'

Garden Flowers

Many automatically think of florists' flowers when planning home displays, but hot-house blooms can seem almost too perfect as well as being expensive to buy. It is possible to raise many of these in your own back yard, where they will grow more as nature intended, as well as simpler flowers with a pleasing informality and charm all their own. These will help you to create more personal arrangements, even if you mix them with a few flowers that you have bought.

Achillea (Asteraceae)

This plant is named for Achilles, a god of the Greeks, who used it medicinally. The Fern-leaf Yarrow (*Achillea filipendula*) has large, plate-like heads packed with lemon flowers and is particularly useful for drying and displaying indoors. Although the yellow variety is dramatic there are others bearing white, pink, red and greenish-white heads. The Achillea can be used in several ways: as a formal display in front of the

Rosa 'La Sevillana'

Rosa 'Blue Moon'

Achillea filipendula

Alstroemeria (Ligtu hybrid)

shiny-green leaves of a beech hedge and in an informal arrangement beside the European Elder (*Sambucus racemosus*).

Alstroemeria (Alstroemeriaceae)
The fleshy and tuberous-rooted Ligtu hybrids grow superbly in warm areas and are excellent for cutting. Popularly known as the Peruvian Lily or Lily-of-the-Incas, this Chilean garden brightener develops masses of trumpet-shaped flowers in pink, scarlet, flame, orange, yellow or white from early to late summer. It is equally as pretty in a mixed bouquet as a country garden, where it will happily mingle with other herbaceous perennials and shrubs.

The roots of this species are used in Chile as a source of starch known locally as *Chuño de Concepción*.

Aster (Asteraceae)
Many Asters that are suitable for cutting and displaying indoors have an all-American ancestry and these include the New England or Fall Asters (*Aster novi-*

Aster novi-belgii

Coreopsis tinctoria

belgii). These produce masses of large, daisy-like flowers in a wide color range during early and mid-fall. The Aster is often known as the Michaelmas Daisy as it flowers around Michaelmas Day, September 29.

Coreopsis (Asteraceae)
Coreopsis tinctoria is another American beauty, with stiff erect stems and masses of clear-yellow flowers shading to brown-red at their centers. It is an ideal candidate for planting alone or in a mixture of other plants. Try arranging it among a medley of annuals, such as the sweetly-scented Nicotiana.

Gaillardia (Asteraceae)
With its bright red-and-yellow daisy-like flowers throughout summer and into mid-fall, the Blanket Flower (*Gaillardia aristata*) is ideal for both borders and vases inside. Few flowers are as dramatic as this all-American beauty, but it tends to dominate neighboring plants, especially those with more demure colors. Therefore, position them in proximity to dramatic flowers with variegated leaves, such as *Phlox paniculata* 'Norah Leigh.'

The Gaillardia was discovered by Captains Meriwether Lewis and William Clark on their celebrated

Gaillardia x grandiflora

journey of 1804–1806, which began soon after the Louisiana Purchase of 1803 in which the United States bought about 828,000 square miles from France for $15 million.

Leucanthemum (Asteraceae)
The Shasta Daisy, now properly known as *Leucanthemum x superbum* but to experienced gardeners as *Chrysanthemum maximum* and commonly as the Max Daisy or Daisy Chrysanthemum, is another totally reliable border plant that floods gardens and graces vases with 3-inch-wide white flowers throughout summer. It is ideal for arranging alongside plants with yellow flowers; two companions could be *Coreopsis verticillata* (page 27) and the Tree Lupin *Lupinus arboreus* (page 37). Alternatively, plant the variegated-leaved *Lamium maculatum* 'Album' in front of the Coreopsis.

Lysimachia (Primulaceae)
The Garden Loosestrife (*Lysimachia punctata*) develops masses of upright stems and this makes it particularly suitable for cutting. It is ideal on its own; alternatively, combine it in a border with the variegated Dogwood (*Cornus alba* 'Spaethii') and *Hosta sieboldiana*, a popular Plantain Lily. Larger species are suitable for damp areas such as bog gardens or pond margins.

Leucanthemum x superbum

Nigella damascena

Lysimachia punctata

Nigella (Ranunculaceae)

With a name like Love-in-a-Mist, *Nigella damascena* is ideal for decorating the table for a romantic meal. It is a hardy annual and the flowers have showy heads surrounded by a smoky froth of finely-cut, bright-green leaves. Although there are varieties with distinctive colors, it is at its best in gardens when sown in large drifts of mixed colors to include shades of mauve, blue, purple and rose-pink.

In the language of flowers it represents perplexity and has been known to gardeners as Love-in-a-Puzzle or Love-Entangled, as well as the more mundane Fennel Flower.

Seeds of the related *Nigella sativa* were used several thousand years ago by Egyptian ladies to induce plumpness which, at that time, was considered to be an attribute of beauty.

Phlox paniculata

Phlox (Polemoniaceae)
Phlox paniculata, widely known as the Fall Phlox, Perennial Phlox or Fall-Flowering Phlox, has a distinctive habit, with large heads composed of sweetly-scented 1-inch flowers from midsummer to early fall. The taller, border Phlox, happiest grown in a moist waterside position, is the most suitable for cutting. It is quite long-lasting in water and will quickly spread its delicious fragrance throughout a room. (See also pages 40–42.)

Reseda (Resedaceae)
If there are gaps in herbaceous borders and you wish to fill them with flowers for cutting, sow the musk-scented annual Mignonette (*Reseda odorata*). It is also ideal for planting in window boxes and growing in beds under windows.

Native to the Mediterranean, it was used to adorn tombs in Egypt in which mummies were laid; but its main claim to fame is through the Empress Josephine, who planted it in her gardens at Malmaison from seeds which her husband, Napoleon Bonaparte, had collected during his Egyptian campaign. Fascination with the plant spread to London, where its exquisite fragrance helped to cloak offensive smells too often apparent in nineteenth-century streets.

Rudbeckia (Asteraceae)
Rudbeckia laciniata, descriptively known as the Coneflower, bears yellow 3–4-inch flowers during late summer and into early fall. Try positioning this plant next to *Leucanthemum x superbum,* still best known as *Chrysanthemum maximum* and popularly as the Shasta Daisy (page 54). The large white flowers create a vibrant feature when mixed with those of the Coneflower and this also applies indoors. The related *Rudbeckia fulgida* (page 42), from the southeastern states, is another spectacular Coneflower, with dome-like, purple-brown centers and yellow to orange flowers.

Reseda odorata

Rudbeckia laciniata

Pretty Potted Plants

Flowering plants already fully established in pots can be bought from florists and garden centers for display in the home. Alternatively, gardeners themselves can raise them in greenhouses and sunrooms. These plants are valuable for creating instant and lasting color, with a range that ensures flowers throughout the year. Winter, perhaps, is the time when color is most welcome, but there are plants suitable for most other seasons. Potted plants include the following all-time winners!

Azalea or Rhododendron (Ericaceae)

One man's Azalea is another's Rhododendron: although Azaleas are now correctly classified as Rhododendrons, to many gardeners the evergreen, small-leaved type grown for decorating homes from Christmas to Easter is still an Azalea. Known at one time as *Azalea indica*, but now *Rhododendron indicum*, plants are grown by specialist nurseries and offered for sale when the buds are starting to open and revealing color. Flowers range from white, pink, salmon-red and dark brick-red to crimson. The clue to success is to keep the compost moist and to avoid drafts and sudden drops in temperature. It is ideal for displaying on a dining or side table, perhaps with the pot standing in a decorative container. Because plants remain in flower for a long time they make an ideal gift, but ensure that they are not exposed to cold during transportation from one location to another.

Calceolaria herbeohybrida

Azalea (Rhododendron indicum)

Calceolaria (Scrophulariaceae)

Calceolaria herbeohybrida is raised from seed each year and is variously known as the Pouch Flower, Slipperwort, Slipper Flower or Pocketbook Flower, from the shape of its flowers. It is a hybrid with several Chilean species in its parentage. As a flowering pot plant, it is available from florists and nurseries from late spring to midsummer. It will also flower outdoors in borders and containers during mid- and late summer. Its oval leaves are soft, slightly hairy, and mid-green, with flowers borne above them in dense clusters in shades of orange, red and yellow. Usually the petals are either blotched or spotted crimson. When buying a plant, check that between half and two-thirds of the flowers are fully developed; situate the plant in a cool, lightly shaded position, keeping the compost moist but not waterlogged. Try displaying this plant at about waist height so that the beautiful flowers are immediately noticed and can be admired.

Cyclamen (Primulaceae)

The Florist's Cyclamen (*Cyclamen persicum*), native to the eastern Mediterranean, has long been popular for decorating homes at Christmas as well as in the preceding few months. The rounded, dark-green leaves are marbled silver, while the distinctive shuttlecock-like flowers are borne above the leaves and at the tops of upright stems. Some strains are fragrant and come in shades of scarlet, white, pink, red and salmon, while others are bicolored or fringed.

The secret of a long progression of flowers is to position the plant in full light and with an ambient temperature of 55–59°F. Keep the compost moist but not waterlogged, and avoid splashing water onto the corm or flowers. Dry air can be a problem, so stand the pot on moist gravel in a decorative saucer. Remove dead flowers by pulling the stem sharply so that it comes away cleanly from the corm. This encourages flowering and reduces the risk of dead flowers spreading decay throughout the plant.

Cyclamen persicum

Euphorbia pulcherrima

Euphorbia (Euphorbiaceae)

The Central American and Mexican plant Poinsettia (*Euphorbia pulcherrima*) is also popularly known in the United States as the Christmas Star, Christmas Flower, Painted Leaf, Lobster Plant or Mexican Flameleaf. In its native habitat it forms a shrub of up to 10 feet, with shallowly-lobed, narrowly-oval, bright-green leaves and flowers that are surrounded by colorful bracts from early to late winter. The leaf-like bracts are usually crimson, although scarlet, pink and white forms are also available.

It is not difficult to grow but a winter temperature of 55–61°F is essential; keep the compost moist but not waterlogged. Avoid cold drafts and place the plant in a well-lit position. Do not crowd it with other plants as its dramatic effect will be spoiled. Many houseplant enthusiasts position Poinsettias on dining tables, side or coffee tables, and on small brass trays that reflect golden light onto the plants. Wall lights nearby will also help flatter them. Like most Euphorbias, Poinsettias contain a white, milky sap which is an irritant to sensitive skins. Take care that it does not get into eyes or cuts and do not swallow.

Hyacinthus (Hyacinthaceae)
Hyacinths (*Hyacinthus orientalis*) are as popular indoors as they are in garden borders. Popularly known as Dutch Hyacinths or Garden Hyacinths, they are invaluable inside, providing scent and color in winter.

Specially-prepared bulbs are essential, with flowers in white, yellow, pink, red and a heavenly range of blues. Bulbs can be planted at home in bowls or pots in early fall and placed in the coolest and darkest place available, perhaps a basement or cellar. Alternatively, bulbs planted earlier at the nursery and already growing can be bought when the flowers are just beginning to show color; if placed in a cool, draft-free and well-lit position, they will create a spectacular display and fragrance for several weeks. Hyacinths are ideal houseplants for positioning in the center of a dining table. When they have finished flowering, do not consign them to the trash can; place them outside in a cool, sheltered position and when all the foliage has died down, plant them among shrubs where they will flower next year.

Hyacinthus orientalis

Hydrangea macrophylla

Hydrangea (Hydrangeaceae)
Florist's Hydrangeas (*Hydrangea macrophylla*) are popular flowering plants for buying in spring, when their large, rounded mop-heads always attract attention. The exact time that they are available depends on the way they have been grown; plants can therefore be bought through to midsummer though some varieties are earlier flowering than others. When grown as garden plants, however, they flower from midsummer to the early fall. Their range is wide and includes many shades of pink and red. By adding "blueing" chemicals to composts, nurserymen can encourage some varieties to produce blue flowers.

Hydrangeas are usually bought when most of the flower heads are fully colored. The size of the plant will be relatively large when compared with the pot, so take care not to let the compost become dry or the plant will topple over.

Justicia (Acanthaceae)
The Shrimp Plant, *Justicia brandegeeana*, still better known as *Beloperone guttata*, is also known as the Shrimp Bush and False Hop. Native to Mexico, it has beautiful shrimp-like flowers from spring to early winter. When in full bloom it is a magnificient sight and deserves a prime position in a room. Because it has a rather relaxed habit, it can be put close to other casual plants. Keep the compost lightly moist and during summer give it a weak feed every ten days.

Kalanchöe (Crassulaceae)
Compared with many other flowering plants, the succulent Flaming Katy (*Kalanchöe blossfeldiana*) is a relative newcomer, but it has become an important florist's favorite. Kalanchöe owes its popularity to its versatility: when young, and by adjusting periods of light and darkness, plants can be brought into bloom throughout the year, and have the added bonus of remaining in flower for seven to eight weeks. The color range of flowers is wide and includes white,

Kalanchöe blossfeldiana

Justicia brandegeeana

pink, red and yellow. Keep it fairly cool (about 41–45°F).

Flaming Katys are resilient plants, but keep the compost slightly moist. Unlike many other houseplants, they look good when three plants are grouped together, perhaps on a window sill or side table. It makes an ideal gift plant as it travels well and creates a display over a long period.

Lilium (Liliaceae)
The Easter Lily (*Lilium longiflorum*), native to Japan and also known in America as the White Lily or Trumpet Lily, is an amenable plant and ideal for growing in a pot and forcing into flower at an earlier time than normal. The trumpet-shaped, heavily-scented white flowers, the golden pollen trembling on long stamens, normally appear during mid- and late summer, but plants can be grown to encourage

flowering in spring for displaying in pots in the house.

The Mid-century Hybrids are ideal for growing in pots and by gentle forcing can be brought into flower at almost any time of the year. Of these, 'Density' is one of the most popular, with lemon-yellow flowers spotted with brown.

As with all Lilies that flower indoors, keep the compost moist but not continually saturated and position the plant in a cool, light room, but not in direct sunlight. Take care that the plant does not get knocked over.

Narcissus (Amaryllidaceae)

To many gardeners, large-faced yellow Daffodils are the epitome of spring, especially when they are naturalized in lawns and on grassy banks. They also bring color to beds under windows, the edges of paths and around shrubs in borders. Plant them lavishly in an out-of-the-way spot in the garden so that they can be used as cut flowers for decorating your home in spring.

Another way is to grow them in pots so that they can be "forced" into flower for Christmas and at other

Lilium longiflorum

Narcissus 'Paper White'

times of the year. Indeed, by using varieties such as 'Soleil d'Or' and 'Paper White' it is possible to have flowers in early winter, but this is the exception; usually, Daffodils are bought growing in pots ready for taking indoors in late winter and early spring. When buying a bowl or pot of Daffodils, check that there are plenty of buds waiting to open, that the compost is evenly moist, and the leaves have not been damaged by pests or diseases. These are robust plants and are ideal for cool rooms, either on lightly-shaded window sills or on side tables.

When the display is over, place the pots outdoors and after the foliage has died down plant the bulbs around shrubs in herbaceous borders.

Pachystachys (Acanthaceae)

The Peruvian Lollipop Plant (*Pachystachys lutea*) makes a flamboyant houseplant and produces cone-shaped yellow bracts with white flower heads from late spring to autumn. Plants dislike drafts and fluctuating temperatures, so avoid positioning them near a window or door. The flowers are enhanced by standing them in a white cachepot; this harmonizes with them and helps to reflect more light onto the plant. If the plant starts to look untidy, place it in a greenhouse or sunroom for a few weeks until it recovers. Keep the compost lightly moist and during summer give it a weak feed every ten to fourteen days.

Pachystachys lutea

Pericallis (Asteraceae)
The popular Cineraria is another houseplant that is raised each year from seed. Now properly called *Pericallis x hybrida* but invariably known as *Cineraria x hybrida,* it is sometimes also referred to as the Florist's Cineraria; it seems to be one of those plants that botanists are always renaming, earlier names being *Cineraria cruenta* and *Senecio cruentus.* (It is well to be aware of previous botanical names as you may have an earlier and treasured gardening book that uses them.) But for gardeners and florists it is the popular name Cineraria that describes this plant, mainly available during spring but also from late fall to early summer. It bears domed heads of flowers in white, lavender, blue, mauve, pink and red. There are also bicolored forms.

When taken indoors, keep the compost moist and position the plant away from cold drafts and strong sunlight. As it forms a domed display, it is ideal for placing on a low table where the flowers can be admired from above.

Pericallis (Cineraria x hybrida)

Schizanthus pinnatus

Schizanthus (Solanaceae)
The South American *Schizanthus pinnatus,* popularly known as the Butterfly Flower or Poor Man's Orchid, is widely grown as a houseplant for flowering during spring and into early summer. It can also be grown to flower outdoors from midsummer to the fall.

Some sixty years ago, the American writers Louise and James Bush-Brown spoke of how the Butterfly Flower reached perfection indoors and was a thing of exquisite beauty. Plants bear small, Orchid-shaped flowers in tones of luminous pink, rose, lavender, purple and yellow, and are attractively marked or spotted. Keep the compost moist, as plants soon wilt when deprived of moisture, causing radical damage to the flowers.

The relaxed nature of the Butterfly Flower makes it ideal for informal rooms rather than grander, more stately ones. It is also better positioned in a corner than in the center of a table where symmetrically-shaped plants are best displayed.

Tulipa (Liliaceae)
Single-early and double-early Tulips are other glorious bulbs which can be encouraged to flower from Christmas to Easter in colors which include scarlet, orange, yellow, vermilion, cherry-red and pink. They can be bought growing in pots or bowls with the buds just beginning to show color. Before purchase, check the compost to ensure that it is moist, as once the roots have been allowed to dry out the bulbs will be quite useless. Make sure that plants are free from pests and diseases. Once indoors, avoid high temperatures and positioning them next to radiators where the air is dry. Keep the compost moist but not waterlogged. Once flowering has finished, plant the bulbs outside.

Tulipa

Flowers for Enthusiasts

Few hobbies are approached with such enthusiasm as gardening. Learning the best way to grow general garden plants, and then specializing in those that you particularly love is most rewarding and an interest that you will wish to communicate to friends. The range of plants which appear to excite special interest is wide and includes Cacti, Chrysanthemums, Dahlias, Lilies, Orchids, Roses and scented-leaved Pelargoniums.

Parodia leninghausii (Notocactus leninghausii)

Cacti

Cacti are among the most popular and fascinating of all indoor plants, not least because they are able to withstand relatively long periods of neglect, which makes them ideal for busy people. Moreover, their range of shapes, sizes and colors make them of interest throughout the year. Cacti belong exclusively to the *Cactaceae* family and are characterized by areoles which resemble small pincushions from which spines, short hooks or long and woolly hairs grow. Flowers and stems also grow from areoles. Another characteristic is that, with the exception of Pereskias and young Opuntias, none of them has leaves; with the exception of Pereskias, all cacti are succulents, or can store water.

Cleistocactus strausii

Cacti are divided into two groups. One of these is the desert type, whose natural environment is in the warm, semi-desert regions of the North American continent. The other is the forest type, which is native to tropical regions of America. However, there is one exception: *Rhipsalis baccifera* is native to Africa and Sri Lanka as well as to America.

Desert types include popular examples such as the Silver Torch (*Cleistocactus strausii*) and the Peanut Cactus (*Echinopsis chamaecereus*, earlier known as *Chamaecereus silvestrii* or *Lobivia silvestrii)*. The most resilient and widely grown Cacti are desert types.

Forest types are easily distinguishable from their desert cousins by their trailing habit and, in some, by their flattened and segmented stems. They often live as epiphytes, attached to trees where they gain support but do not take nourishment from the host. Forest Cacti include plants such as the Christmas Cactus and Easter Cactus (both with flattened and segmented stems) and the popular Rat's Tail Cactus (*Aporocactus flagelliformis*).

Before buying Cacti, thoroughly check them out. Cacti tend to be specialist plants and are usually sold through reputable nurseries and garden centers. Each plant should be clearly labeled and free from pests and diseases. Do not buy plants with algae or slime on top of the compost or on the pot; this is unsightly and indicates that the plant has been neglected. Do not buy plants that are displayed outside shops in winter: although most desert Cacti prefer low temperatures during winter, cold winds and unpredictable low temperatures can soon kill them off. Moreover, cold shocks to forest Cacti may cause flower buds to fall off or not to open properly.

Some Cacti are more easily grown than others; here are ten desert types that are ideal for beginners.

Ball Cactus (*Parodia leninghausii*, earlier known as *Notocactus leninghausii*): Also known as the Golden Ball Cactus, it forms a cylindrical, light-green stem with white wool at the top. It is slow-growing and throughout summer displays golden-yellow flowers of about 1 inch wide.

Barrel Cactus (*Echinocactus grusonii*): Also known as Golden Ball and Golden Barrel Cactus, it is a slow-growing, barrel-shaped Cactus with many ribs and golden-yellow spines. During late spring, old and large plants bear tubular yellow flowers, each about 3 inches across.

Fire-Crown Cactus (*Rebutia senilis*): The spherical, pale-green stem bears tiny bright-red flowers during late spring and early summer. It has white spines and is ideal for growing on a window sill.

Fish-Hook Cactus (*Mammillaria bocansana*): Also known as the Powder-Puff Cactus and Snowball Cactus, it has a blue-green body with fine white spines and silky hairs. During early summer it bears cream flowers. Eventually the Cactus will form a cushion-like clump, up to 6 inches across.

Opuntia microdasys

Echinocactus grusonii

Golden Column (*Echinopsis spachiana*, earlier known as *Trichocereus spachianus*): Also known as Torch Cactus and White Torch Cactus, it has bright green stems up to 12 inches high, with short spines. Plants often branch from the base and when large bear large, greenish-white flowers which open at night.

Peanut Cactus (*Echinopsis chamaecereus*, earlier known as *Chamaecereus silvestrii* or *Lobivia silvestrii*): Bright-green, finger-like stems with short spines. Plants produce offsets that are similar to green peanuts, and during spring and summer develop brilliant scarlet flowers.

Prickly Pear (*Opuntia microdasys*): Also known as Bunny-Ears, Rabbit-Ears, Cholla Cactus or Goldplush, this is a widely-grown Cactus with a much-branched and bushy habit. It develops pale-green, oval, spineless pads, each up to 6 inches long. It rarely produces flowers when in cultivation, but it is nevertheless well worth growing in a pot indoors or in a desert garden in a greenhouse or sunroom.

Rat's-Tail Cactus (*Aporocactus flagelliformis*): Although a forest Cactus, it is better grown as a desert type and planted in a pot positioned on a shelf near a window. Stems up to 2 feet long and 1/2 an inch thick bear magenta, funnel-shaped flowers up to 3 inches wide in spring.

Sea-Urchin Cactus (*Echinopsis aurea*): Sometimes listed as *Lobivia aurea*, it has cylindrical ribbed stems about 4 inches long and short spines. Lemon-yellow flowers appear in spring and summer.

Silver Torch Cactus (*Cleistocactus strausii*): This plant forms a tall, slender column smothered in short, white spines that give the plant a silvery gleam. Large and mature plants bear carmine flowers during mid- and late summer.

Some desert Cacti have a more demanding nature. Here are five of them:

Ball Cactus (*Parodia haselbergii*, earlier known as *Notocactus haselbergii*): Also known as the Scarlet Ball Cactus, it forms a globular or cylindrical bright-green body with yellow-white spines. Bright orange-red flowers appear during spring and early summer.

Rebutia fiebrigii (muscula)

Cephalocereus senilis

Bishop's Mitre (*Astrophytum myriostigma*): Also known as Bishop's-Cap Cactus or Monkshood, it forms a cylindrical plant with dark-green skin smothered in silvery scales. The number of ribs varies, but is usually four to eight. Throughout summer, sweetly-scented, pale-yellow flowers appear at the top of the plant.

Cob Cactus (*Echinopsis kuehnrichii*, earlier known as *Lobivia densispina*): A small, clump-forming plant with individual heads about 2 inches long. They are covered in whitish spines along the ribs. Yellow flowers occur in clusters at the top of each head during summer. There are also varieties with orange, pink or red flowers.

Crown Cactus (*Rebutia fiebrigii*, earlier known as *Rebutia muscula*): Clump-forming, with pale-green stems about 2 inches across, and masses of soft, white spines. During late spring and early summer it bears orange flowers.

Fish-Hook Cactus (*Ferocactus cylindraceus*, earlier known as *Ferocactus acanthodes*): This Cactus has a fierce appearance, with sharp, tough spines, hooked at their ends. Small plants do not bear flowers, but when blooming does occur the flowers are pale-yellow.

A few Cacti are even more difficult to grow, and these include:

Glory-of-Texas (*Thelocactus bicolor*): Distinctively, the globular stems and ribs divide into notches, with red spines that reveal amber tips. It does not always flower, but when it does the flowers are violet-red.
Old Man Cactus (*Cephalocereus senilis*): One of the most distinctive and popular Cacti. In its native Mexico (and after about 200 years) it forms a column 40 feet high! It has a pale-green stem with yellow spines, completely hidden by long, white hairs. Unfortunately, the white flowers do not appear on small plants.
Sand-Dollar Cactus (*Astrophytum asterias*): Also known as Sand-Dollar Cactus, Sea-Urchin Cactus, Silver-Dollar or Star Cactus, it forms a flattened, apple-green sphere with eight broad, shallow ribs marked with white scales. Yellow flowers appear throughout summer, even on young plants.

Border Chrysanthemum

Chrysanthemum 'Ryestar'

Chrysanthemum (Asteraceae)
The well-known Florist's Chrysanthemums which both professional and amateur gardeners have enjoyed growing in gardens and greenhouses for more than 100 years are perhaps the most popular flowers to be cultivated by enthusiasts. The range of types is wide and includes the Outdoor Chrysanthemums (also known as Border Chrysanthemums and Early-flowering Chrysanthemums) and Greenhouse Chrysanthemums (also known as Late-flowering Chrysanthemums).

Outdoor Chrysanthemums offer the choice of Small-flowered types that require little attention except for "stopping" (removing the terminal bud in early summer) and Decorative types with larger flowers that need stopping and support with canes and strings. Disbudding (removing the side buds) is not usually necessary. In addition there are the Decorative types grown to produce flowers for cutting and room decoration. For these, both stopping and disbudding are essential. They also need support from canes.

Dahlia 'Wootton Impact'

Greenhouse types include flowering pot plants which are usually Dwarf varieties as well as Charm varieties. Stopping may be necessary, but not disbudding. However, the most popular greenhouse chrysanthemums are the Decoratives. Decorative Chrysanthemums grown in greenhouses are the type frequently favored by enthusiasts. Within this group there are Incurved varieties, which have flowers with florets that turn towards the center, thereby creating the impression of a ball. Intermediate varieties have a looser and more irregular nature, with both incurved and reflexed petals. Reflexed types have florets that turn outwards and downwards.

Decorative Chrysanthemums are the ones that inspire the most competition among enthusiasts, which is not surprising when one remembers that monster flowers result, each up to 10 inches wide.

Dahlia (Asteraceae)

Dahlias have long been popular flowers in the United States, and over the years a vast range of types have been developed; the American Dahlia Society recognizes 12 distinct groups. It is unlikely that there will be a further large development of Dahlias in the future except, perhaps, in their range of colors. However, it is possible that the southern Mexico and Central American species *D. imperialis* may have a greater impact. Known as the Bell Tree Dahlia, Candelabra Dahlia or Tree Dahlia, it grows to 20 feet, with white, red-centered flowers and is an herbaceous to woody perennial.

Lilium (Liliaceae)

Lilies have a long history of domestication and were pictured on Cretan vases as early as 2500–1500 BC. There are about 80 species scattered around the northern hemisphere, in places including the United States, Europe, Russia, China and Japan. Popular Lilies grown in the United States include:

***L. aurantum*:** This belongs to the Oriental group which includes several spectacular types such as the Japanese Golden-Rayed Lily, known in America as the Golden-Banded Lily of Japan, Golden-Banded Lily or Mountain Lily. Native to Japan and widely acclaimed as the Queen of the Lilies, it has fragrant, bowl-shaped, brilliant white flowers with golden-yellow rays or bands during late summer and into the early fall. Each flower is up to 12 inches across, with purple or wine-colored spots on the inner surfaces of each petal.

***L. canadensis*:** This has several popular names including the Canada Lily, Meadow Lily, Wild Meadow Lily, Wild Yellow Lily, Yellow Bell Lily or Yellow Lily. In the 1800s, the Irish-born American garden writer Bernard McMahon referred to this as the Canada

Dahlia 'Biddenham Purple'

Lilum aurantum

Martagon Lily, and, although other writers refer to it as the Swamp Lily, it certainly will not flourish in waterlogged soil. During midsummer it bears pendent, bell-shaped yellow or red-orange flowers spotted brown or purple-red. Lime-free soil and full sun or partial shade suit it best.

***L. candidum*:** The Madonna Lily from Asia Minor is one of the most popular of all and is claimed to be the oldest domesticated flower. Also known as the Annunciation Lily, Bourbon Lily or White Lily, it is often featured in Renaissance paintings, usually in association with the Virgin Mary. During early and mid-summer it bears fragrant, trumpet-shaped white flowers with golden pollen. Although it is often difficult to establish and resents disturbance, it is nevertheless well worth growing.

***L. michiganense*:** The Michigan Lily is closely related to the Canada Lily and comes from central and eastern states of America. It is a meadow flower, grows best in full sunlight, and has a graceful appearance with orange-red flowers spotted reddish-maroon, with a green basal spot.

***L. pardalinum*:** The Leopard Lily, sometimes known as the Panther Lily, also dislikes acid soil and is native to California, consequently enjoying plenty of sun. It is easily grown and during midsummer produces orange-red, Turk's-Cap-like flowers with light orange-yellow centers dotted with purple or orange-brown. The form 'Giganteum,' known as the Sunset Lily, has larger and more robust flowers, with deep golden centers and vermilion petals.

***L. philadelphicum*:** The Flame Lily is native to North America where it is also known as the Wood Lily, Orange Cup Lily or Wild Orange-Red Lily. It is said to be difficult to grow away from its native home, which is unfortunate since the upward-facing, cup-shaped,

Lilium pardalinum

Lilium regale

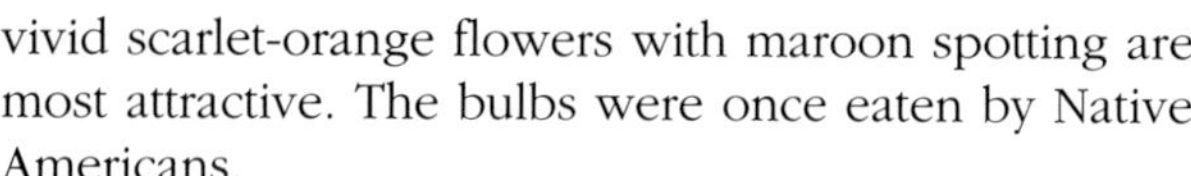

vivid scarlet-orange flowers with maroon spotting are most attractive. The bulbs were once eaten by Native Americans.

***L. pyrenaicum*:** The yellow Turk's-Cap Lily is native to the Pyrenees and is valuable for its early flowering, when it bears pendulous bright-yellow flowers with purple-black spots and orange-red pollen.

***L. regale*:** The Regal Lily, known in America as the Royal Lily, is a trumpet type with fragrant, funnel-shaped flowers with sulfur-yellow centers, each up to 5 inches long, during midsummer.

***L. speciosum*:** Native to Japan, this is known in America as the Showy Lily, Japanese Lily or Showy Japanese Lily. It develops fragrant, bowl-shaped white flowers, each up to 2 inches long, in late summer and into early fall. The nodding flowers are heavily shaded with crimson. 'Stargazer' is derived from this species.

***L. superbum*:** This is native to the eastern states and widely known as the American Turk's-Cap Lily, Lily-Royal or Swamp Lily, the latter being an indication of its natural preference for moist areas. During mid- and late summer it bears nodding 4-inch-wide orange-scarlet flowers, spotted with purplish-brown, the vivid red anthers adding to the display. Native Americans are reputed to have once added the bulbs to soups.

Orchids (Orchidaceae)

Few flowers are surrounded by such an aura of mystique as Orchids, with their often intricate, delicate and waxy appearance. The Orchid family is one of the largest in the plant kingdom, with about 750 different genera, at least 25,000 native species, and more than 30,000 cultivated hybrids.

Orchid flowers are dramatic and distinctive, with an unusual structure and their own vocabulary. Although in size they range from minute types to those with 8-inch-wide flowers, they all have the same basic construction. Each has three sepals (the outermost parts of a flower) and three petals. In most other flowers, the sepals are leaf-like and green and protect the unopened flower. With Orchids they are colorful and an intricate part of the flower; the uppermost one is slightly larger than the other two.

Orchids are celebrated for their flamboyant flowers,

but some are also famous for their fragrance. Most are just sweet-smelling, but others have unusual and distinctive scents that range from almond to musk and newly-mown hay. A few have a commercial role and at one time none more so than *Vanilla planifolia.* The warm, luxurious bouquet and flavor of vanilla is derived from pods produced by this large, creeping Orchid. It demands warmth and high rainfall, although it does need a dry season to encourage the pods to ripen. A related Orchid, *Vanilla pompona*, produces inferior-quality vanilla, although it is claimed to have advantages over *V. planifolia* in that the pods are thicker and shorter and not as likely to split at the ends. Plants are also claimed to flower and fruit more or less throughout the year.

There are two main groups of Orchids: terrestrial types which grow at ground level and are rooted in soil, and epiphytes, which live perched on trees and shrubs,

Dendrobium 'Utopia'

Lilium speciosum

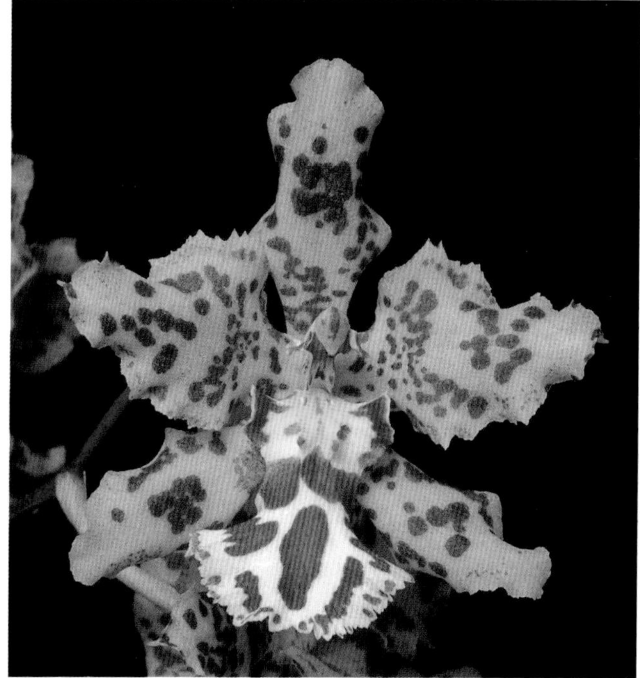

Odontoglossum grande

not as parasites but merely elevated above the forest floor. They use their host for support and anchorage and usually grow on dead plant debris at the junctions of branches. Their roots draw moisture and nourishment from the debris.

Terrestrial Orchids usually live in temperate regions, while epiphytic forms are chiefly found in tropical and subtropical locations, and it is these that are mainly grown indoors or in greenhouses.

As well as using the entire plant to decorate greenhouses, sunrooms and window sills, flower spikes can be cut off and displayed in vases indoors. Severing them from the plant at the right time is important: this should preferably be done when the terminal flower has been open for at least ten days. Cut the stem at its base and place the spike in fresh, clean water and in a cool position out of direct sunlight and away from cold drafts. Every few days, cut a thin slice off the base of the stem and renew the water. Rather than severing the stem straight across, cut it at a slant. It is essential not to crush the stem as this blocks the passage of water and reduces the life of the flower.

Another way of using Orchids is to combine them with other flowers to produce attractive corsages and buttonholes. Combining an Orchid, such as a Dendrobium or Phalaenopsis, with Stephanotis flowers and a few variegated leaves creates a magnificent display. Before making a corsage, place the stem of the Orchid overnight in clean water. When complete, the corsage can be kept fresh for a few days by placing it in a plastic container in the refrigerator.

There are many Orchids from which to choose and some of the easiest to grow include:

***Cattleya aurantiaca*:** This is one of the smallest Cattleyas, with drooping clusters of red-orange flowers, each 3–4 inches wide, during summer.

***Dendrobium nobile*:** One of the most popular cool-growing Dendrobiums, it is ideal for window sills where from midwinter to spring it bears attractive flowers, rosy-purple at the ends of the petals and shading to white towards the centers. Each lip has a rich maroon blotch at its throat. There are more than 80 varieties in a wide range of colors.

***Lycaste deppei*:** This is a robust Orchid, with flowers of up to 4 inches wide during late winter and spring, and sometimes into early summer. Each flower has mid-green sepals spotted reddish-brown, and small, pure-white petals. The lip is yellow and spotted reddish-brown.

***Odontoglossum grande*:** An ideal plant for a greenhouse as well as on window sills indoors, where the plants bear four to seven 6-inch-wide flowers on 12-inch stems from late summer to early winter. The sepals and petals are bright yellow and marked with chestnut-brown.

***Paphiopedilum venustum*:** A distinctive plant, with leaves heavily marbled grey and green. One, or occasionally, two flowers, each about 3 inches across, are borne on stems up to 9 inches long during winter and often into spring. The petals and lips are yellow-green, tinged rose-red, while the sepal at the back is white and strongly striped with green.

***Pleione bulbocodioides*:** Previously and still popularly known as *P. formosana*, this is ideal for growing in both a greenhouse and indoors where from midwinter to late spring it bears pure white to deep mauve-pink flowers. The lips of the flowers are fringed and crested, and spotted ginger or brick-red.

Rosa (Rosaceae)

American rose enthusiasts invariably like to grow a range of roses and nursery catalogs offer Wild Roses as well as Old Roses, which encompass the Albas, Bourbons, Damasks, Gallicas, Hybrid Musks, Hybrid

Rosa gallica 'Versicolor'

Rosa virginiana

Perpetuals, Hybrid Rugosas, Hybrid Sweetbriars, Moss, Portland and Scotch Roses. Some of these Roses have the bonus of fragrances that will amaze, such as the raspberry-like scent of the Bourbon Roses 'Adam Masserich' and 'Honorine de Brabant.' Or the clover-like perfume of the Modern Shrub Rose 'Fritz Nobis' and the sweet-pea scent of the Hybrid Musk 'Vanity.' These and many others are a source of infinite pleasure.

Several Roses are native to the United States and many experts like to grow a selection of all-American types. Here are a few that will beautify your garden:

***R. californica*:** The California Wild Rose is indigenous from southern Oregon to Baja California and bears clusters of carmine-pink flowers during early and mid-summer. These are followed in the fall by round, red fruits known as hips or heps, also known as *macuatas,* and are eaten cooked or raw, having first been sweetened by frost.

***R. carolina*:** Another native American grown from Maine to Florida, this is known as the Swamp Rose. The plant puts out suckers and during early and mid-summer reveals light-pink flowers.

***R. gymnocarpa*:** This is the Redwood Rose or Wood Rose from the western part of the United States and has a pretty and graceful appearance, with rosy-pink flowers up to 2 inches wide.

***R. laevigata*:** This is commonly known as the Cherokee Rose, so it is difficult to consider it as anything other than an American native. However, its home area is wide and includes Southern China, Taiwan and Indochina. It is claimed that the single, 3–4-inch fragrant, pure-white flowers are the most beautiful of all the single Roses. They appear above glossy-green leaves.

***R. virginiana*:** The Dwarf Wild Rose from the eastern part of America has a thicket-forming habit with clusters of pink flowers during mid- and late summer. It has the bonus of attractive red or orange fruits.

Rosa rugosa 'Frau Dagmar Hastrup'

Scented-Leaved Pelargonium (Geraniaceae)
Also known as scented-leaved Geraniums, these are popular enthusiast plants, both indoors and in greenhouses as well as outdoors when the climate permits. They are tender, soft-stemmed shrubs which botanically are Pelargoniums rather than Geraniums. The range of fragrances that can be produced even in a small area is remarkably large and these distinctive plants soon become a passion, with scents ranging from apple to lavender and ginger. Plants are quickly damaged by frost and low temperatures and during winter they need a minimum temperature of 45°F and as much sunlight as possible. Do not mist-spray the leaves as they may be damaged.

There are many scented-leaved Pelargoniums in a wide range of fragrances. Here are some to look for.

Almond-scented leaves
***Pelargonium quercifolium* (Almond Geranium/Oak-leaved Geranium/Village-Oak**

Pelargonium quercifolium

Geranium): This is a well-branched but erect plant with toothed edges and lobed mid-green leaves that emit an almond fragrance with a hint of balsam when bruised. It has pink flowers with deep-purple veins and blooms from spring to early summer and often later.

Apple-scented leaves

***Pelargonium odoratissimum* (Apple Geranium/Apple-scented Geranium):** A low-growing and somewhat sprawling plant with trailing stems and light-green, velvety, round- to heart-shaped leaves that have a fragrance of ripe apples when bruised. It has white flowers from late spring to mid-summer.

Apricot- and lemon-scented leaves

***Pelargonium scabrum* (Apricot Geranium/Strawberry Geranium):** This is an erect plant with deeply-lobed, rough-surfaced and hairy leaves that emit an apricot fragrance with a strong hint of lemon when bruised. It has white to pink or pinkish-purple flowers during spring and summer.

Balsam-scented leaves

***Pelargonium denticulatum* 'Filicifolium' (Fern-leaf Geranium/Pine Geranium):** An upright plant, with sticky, rough-surfaced, triangular and segmented leaves which emit a balsam-like fragrance when bruised. It has purple-pink flowers from spring to midsummer and sometimes later.

Eucalyptus-scented leaves

***Pelargonium* 'Clorinda':** Distinctive, with three-lobed, green leaves that reveal a Eucalyptus-like fragrance when bruised. Some people can detect a Cedar-like scent. It develops rose-pink flowers with the upper petals streaked purple during spring and throughout summer.

Ginger-scented leaves

***Pelargonium* 'Torento':** A compact plant with leaves which emit the fragrance of ginger and citrus when bruised. It has large, mauve-pink flowers in late spring and summer.

Lavender-scented leaves

***Pelargonium dichondrifolium* (Lavender Geranium):** Also occasionally known as *P. cradockense*, it has grey-green leaves which emit the fragrance of lavender when bruised. It has white flowers marked with red lines during summer.

Pelargonium x fragrans 'Creamy Nutmeg'

Lemon- and citron-scented leaves

***Pelargonium crispum* (Lemon Geranium):** Slender, and well-branched, this upright plant has green, hoary, deeply-lobed leaves which have a rich lemon and balm-like fragrance when bruised. The rose-pink flowers appear during spring and summer.

***Pelargonium crispum* 'Major' (Finger-bowl Geranium):** Upright plant with small, green, crisp-edged leaves which give out a sweet, citron-like fragrance when bruised. It has pale-mauve or pink flowers in spring and throughout summer.

Lime-scented leaves

***Pelargonium* 'Nervosum' (Lime Geranium/Lime-scented Geranium):** Sometimes listed as *Pelargonium nervosum*, it has small, dark-green leaves with sharply toothed edges which emit a lime-like fragrance when bruised. It has lavender flowers marked with purple from spring to mid summer.

Nutmeg-scented leaves

***Pelargonium x fragrans* (Nutmeg Geranium):** This is well-branched, with grey-green, velvety, three-lobed leaves which emit a nutmeg and pine fragrance when bruised. It has small white flowers prominently veined and spotted in red from spring to mid-summer.

Orange-scented leaves

***Pelargonium* 'Prince of Orange' (Orange Pelargonium):** An erect plant, it has small, light-green leaves which emit an orange-like scent when buised. It has large, pale-mauve flowers during summer.

Peppermint-scented leaves

***Pelargonium* 'Chocolate Peppermint':** This has large, lobed leaves with central brown blotches; when the leaves are bruised they give off a peppermint-like bouquet. It has small pink flowers during summer.

***Pelargonium* 'Joy Lucille':** Attractive grey-green, deeply-cut leaves which emit a peppermint fragrance when bruised. The white flowers are tinged with mauve.

***Pelargonium tomentosum* (Mint Geranium/Herb-scented Geranium/Peppermint Geranium):** A hummock-forming and slightly prostrate plant with pale-green, soft and hairy leaves with white undersides. When bruised they give off a strong peppermint smell. The white flowers are peppered red in summer.

Rose-scented leaves

***Pelargonium graveolens* (Rose-scented Geranium/Rose Geranium):** Also known as Pelargonium 'Graveolens,' this is widely-grown with a branching habit and hoary green, deeply-lobed leaves which have a sweet and Rose-like fragrance when bruised. It has rose-pink flowers with dark purple spots during summer.

Pelargonium 'Clorinda'

Index

Index